We are advocat

principles of thi

professionally. Here are some of their comments:

"Brandie is a thoughtful leader. Her techniques inspire organizational and people excellence. Her challenge phrase 'BY WHEN' drives her readers to results."

— Cindy, Human Resources, Iowa

"The words 'BY WHEN' never had very much meaning to me until I met Brandie Hinen. I never knew that two words would change the way I did everything and defined what my expectations should be of others. I learned that providing a 'BY WHEN' that it was the key to getting an answer to a request."

— Consuelo, Education Director, New Mexico

"When Brandie speaks, she has the ability to engage others through both her personal stories and tidbits of wisdom, and this book is no exception. Her 'BY WHEN' concept has completely changed the way I communicate professionally and has also helped me manage my expectations, and I find myself using her tools often. Because her advice can be applied to any level, profession or industry, this is not a book I would read just once - it is truly a resource I know I will refer back to often."

— Allison, Marketing, Virginia

"Brandie's 'BY WHEN' and 'Commited to Create' advice helped me tremendously in my life as a professional writer/editor and in my most important relationships. Learners Kick Butt, and so I keep learning from Brandie's methods. This is the sort of boot camp that I need as a creative person—and make no mistake, Brandie herself is an unstoppable creative force for good!"

— Kristin, California

"'BY WHEN' has changed the way I hold myself and my team accountable. Brandie's methods have transformed procrastination and distraction into positive progression. BY WHEN is exceptional and empowering."

— Drew, Marketing, Nebraska

"Brandie offers a no-nonsense approach to increasing productivity in the workplace and beyond with 'BY WHEN'. She has a brilliant way of cutting through the noise that keeps people stuck and unable to meet personal and professional goals. 'BY WHEN' delivers a practical and easy-to-follow method for putting the wheels of a plan in motion and overcoming common traps that road block success."

— Aimee, Author, California

"When I first heard about Brandie and Powerhouse Learning, I was skeptical this type of change would transform my operation. Boy was that an understatement. Brandie has helped me simplify my operation by helping me think through practical ways of achieving our goals. Her 'BY WHEN' method and getting 'Agreement' from my staff has helped changed the morale and helped streamline our processes."

— Chris, CEO/Entrepreneur, South Carolina

"Brandie's 'BY WHEN' has penetrated our company and almost every organization I am involved with in an advisory capacity; it creates clarity of expectations, has improved follow through, and has eliminated the stress of not knowing and questioning when/if the item will be done."

— Chris, Vice President, Kansas

"Brandie's brilliant philosophy has been instrumental in creating a easy to follow mentality that yields immediate results. I have seen the results and coordination amongst my coworkers and my family by setting into motion the simple philosophy of 'BY WHEN'. Thank you for making my world a much more productive one."

— Vivian, Sales, New Mexico

"Brandie's 'BY WHEN' method will help you to obtain your desired results in your professional and personal life. Her intuition and direction on interactions in the workplace and life are spot on. She has inspired me and I know will do the same for you!"

— Alexia, Regional Director, Arizona

BY WHEN

Moving Discussion
into Action

How to get what you want when you want it

Brandie J. Hinen

Powerhouse Learning

BY WHEN
Copyright © 2018 Brandie J. Hinen

ISBN 13: 978-0-9996412-0-0
IBSN 10: 0999641204

Powerhouse Learning
www.powerhouselearning.com

Cover and interior design by Tugboat Design, LLC - www.tugboatdesign.net
Editing by Kristin Johnson - www.kristinjohnson.net
Illustrations by Juan Ramón Morales - info@diseniarte.com

"You know it seems like such a simple thing, that two very basic words can have so much meaning and so much connotation in both work lives and personal lives.

BY WHEN changes the face of things. It is the daily triumph of integrity over skepticism.

It gives people hope, deadlines, a place to stand and know that progress is in progress!"

– Brandie Hinen

Contents

Introduction

I grew up in the South. Not the Deep South but Houston, Texas. My mother remarried when I was four or five to my stepfather, a supervisor for offshore drilling rigs. We packed up and moved every two years, yet made our way back to our home base, Houston, every time we returned to the States for a new assignment. Although our migratory patterns resembled those of many military families, we didn't enjoy the luxury of being in community like the military. We lived "in country" and in what we now call "developing countries," which everyone called Third World countries then, throughout my childhood during the 1970s.

With each relocation, I got a crash course in the native language. In Venezuela I absorbed Spanish; a move to Brazil introduced me to Portuguese (a country and people I adore to this day); in West Africa, I learned French. We also spent time in the Netherlands, Antilles and Trinidad & Tobago.

Further, even when we found the place where we lived difficult, we faced the inevitability of moving somewhere else at a moment's notice. We toggled from huge cities like Rio de Janeiro to the Amazon rainforest with jungle on three sides of our house, to urban Abidjan, then, ultimately, back to the United States to a very small, isolated farm community of 1500 people (including the surrounding population). The change marked the ugliest and most awkward time for me as a twelve-year-old girl. I had to abandon the diversity of overseas living for the uniformity of a country lifestyle.

My stepfather, who grew up on a farm in Canada, decided to settle in rural Idaho, on a homestead that featured some acreage on the Snake River, so that I would learn the rural work ethic. My standard chores included handpicking rocks on forty acres while my stepfather operated the truck. Over time, I learned how to move sprinkler pipe, work with cattle, and much to my enjoyment, began riding then starting horses. Working with horses served as my great escape for much of my life afterwards.

After high school I left Idaho and vowed never to return. Looking for a lifestyle similar to what I had during my (mostly) urban upbringing, I spent most of my business career in both Southern and Northern California.

But my love of learning never subsided; my ravenous appetite for books, seminars, trainings, anything I could get my hands on, started around the age of twelve and stuck with me. I combined that love of knowledge with an insatiable curiosity about what makes people tick, what makes them do the things they do, how they make decisions, and what ultimately leads them to achieving or not achieving their heart's desire.

In June of 1996, while living in Santa Rosa, California, I went through a four-day experiential training workshop that radically changed my life by giving me a foundation for learning how to understand people, and to look at myself in the mirror. That experience taught me *the difference between who I was vs. who I said I was* and I faced some harsh realities in the disparity during that workshop and afterwards.

During that same seminar, I learned one of the most powerful principles I know, one that still guides my work today: "If my vision was powerful enough to call me through the pain of transformation, I would change." Later, I served on teams as part of the organization that sponsored the seminar and learned much about our human condition—the perfect supplement to my obsessive nature on the subject.

I experienced a complete shift, and despite all my earlier protests when I left Idaho, I came back in 2000 for a welcome change and to raise my children and instill the best values I could.

Fast forward to 2003, when, at the age of thirty-three, I received requests to work with businesses both in and outside of the commercial insurance industry. My prior experience as a successful producer in Northern California and as a VP of Marketing for a five-location firm provided the bedrock for my credibility in the field. As a young business coach, I gathered tons of experience working with and learning from the challenges that organizations face working with customers, prospects, vendors, and of course, staff. Those challenges ranged from front desk employees to big hairy partnership conflicts and blow-ups. I worked with banks, hospitals, non-profits, real estate development, hospitality, and others—all before I turned forty!

Throughout these corporate engagements, I began to make a name for myself in industry circles. In 2006, my reputation as an implementer of change earned me a spot on the faculty for a national training organization. My coaching and consulting career took off as well and dumped me right in the middle of the deep end of the pool of human conflict, family business in-fighting, difficult business situations the likes of which I had never seen or thought existed. (Predicaments that were so harrowing that I'm not even able to share many situations with you.) I also helped nonprofits resolve internal conflicts and reaffirm the vision behind their good works. Suffice it to say, I landed at the center of living my vision, giving to my work everything that I had through my passion, and desperately trying to find my own identity of what I would stand for and what I would not.

The exposure to such varied organizational problems in such a short period of time and across several industries might have been too much for many people. With my insatiable desire for change and experience, I needed this fast-paced ever-changing environment to soak up the human experience and hone my interpersonal skills and insightfulness. The beautiful thing about being asked to come in and help bring perspective to other people's difficulties is that it forced me to problem-solve, think on my feet, and understand how to move a culture in thirty seconds or less. Okay, maybe not literally, but the expectation of those who finally hire outside help can be pretty steep! Companies will not wait around for you to get up to speed. Issues come quickly and if you can't diagnose the problem within that tight expectation window and move toward a solution, the consulting gig may not be for you.

While my business flourished and I felt Committed to Create greatness with every encounter, I soon realized on many occasions that I would want what I called IT (change) more than my customers would want IT. I gave so much of myself because I labored under the delusion that my desire for change would be powerful enough to drive the client when he or she lacked internal resources. After all, that is what they were paying me for, right?

Now that I have more years and experience under my belt,

I have developed little triggers or life hacks to help me gauge whether someone is really serious and willing to do their part to begin the process of radical change. You'll discover that those life hacks include giving homework, using Conversations for Action (C4A) and my infamous BY WHENs.

I'll share a secret with you: People readily talk about what they want to change to a coach like me. But that doesn't mean much until clients demonstrate willingness to DO something about it. Until they face their fears and insecurities, and the demons of the past failures, talk is all we got, *capisce*? Only though the pain does breakthrough come. Only after failure comes success. We should be willing to risk failure AGAIN to succeed. There is no other way, really.

I served as the accountability my clients lacked, mixed with enough compassion and concern to challenge their efforts and to help them make a commitment to change, to demand, and to know BY WHEN. ☺

I've contributed a lot of my experiences, life lessons, client advice, and stories to this book in hopes that those I can't reach personally can benefit from my experience. To me this book represents a simple way to get a clear message across, chiefly that "Action Drives Results," as well as all the practical life challenges that people have valued over the years.

After over ten years of being asked to create a written work, I have chosen (with a little help from some amazingly talented and pushy friends who cared enough about me to hold me accountable and help me overcome my greatest insecurity) to share some of my personal stories and life lessons with all of you. I thank you for listening.

How To Use this Book

How to Use This Book, or Orange Juice vs. Kool-Aid

Disclaimer: This book delivers straight talk and authenticity. In reading BY WHEN, you'll get what I call "orange juice versus Kool-Aid." I borrowed that term from my mother-in-law. She's a wise woman who has much life experience and she says there are two kinds of people: There are people who like orange juice and there are people who like Kool-Aid. One group appreciates authenticity and value. The other enjoys food coloring and fake sugar.

This book is fresh squeezed and all natural. Likely with a little pulp. Free of clichés.

My commitment is to bring you real-life information, real-life language and things you can use starting today. I'm sharing my favorite life principles that you can start using right now, the things that have made an impact on my life over the years, and some original insights.

I named my company Powerhouse Learning in homage of the enormous energy that a powerhouse efficiently generates. Gears in a powerhouse are designed to give you the most power with the least amount of effort. For me, this means that you can use the material in the pages of BY WHEN to balance your thinking ability and skills with your heart's discernment of truth. Take what works and leave the rest. If something bothers you, affects you, causes you to question what I'm saying, please go do the research – get on the Internet. It's a powerful thing.

Look inside yourself. Find out where you need to do some work and please do the work. Be willing to do the hardest thing to get the greatest result in life.

Who Can Use This Book

This book is created for those that are ready for the how-tos. You are tired of listening to instructors or speakers give you just enough content and yet probably leave you more confused than you were when you came into the room, watched the DVD or listened to the CD/Webcast. This book is for the people who know that one of the best things you can do for yourself and for those around you is to be engaged in learning.

BY WHENS In Each Chapter, or Why Good Coaches Give Homework

At the end of each chapter, and in the chapters themselves, you will find exercises to help you practice your personal BY WHENS.

I hear you saying, "Oh, no, homework!" Cue the eye rolls and deep sighs.

Why do I give homework?

As a business coach that likes to get down to core problems and witness incredible results through the way that we create language, I have found a secret breakthrough by giving assignments for staff to work on.

In my opinion, homework really helps create an opening and a space where team members get to think about the situation at hand and come up with valuable fixes. I believe that team members are focused on solving problems for the customer every day; they use their wit, insight, experience, and graduate degrees in the School of Hard Knocks many times, several times a day to do amazing things in business. I believe they have the same capability to help overcome organizational challenges. Sending a staff member away to think about a challenge or an issue helps the team because they are using problem solving skills used for the customer then to help support the health and strategic initiatives for the team.

What does homework really do? I think it helps employees come up with solutions to their own problems. When we ask staff members to give us information back, it allows them to help contribute in ways that we often would not have considered. I think having conversation in this way allows people to:

- Remove themselves from things for a moment
- Engage in the situation with a new set of eyes
- Bring discipline to a scenario
- Think about the results the staff member would like to have
- Helps build character
- Brings learning to a situation where an employee or staff member may actually feel stuck.

SECTION I

14 Personal Change Principles

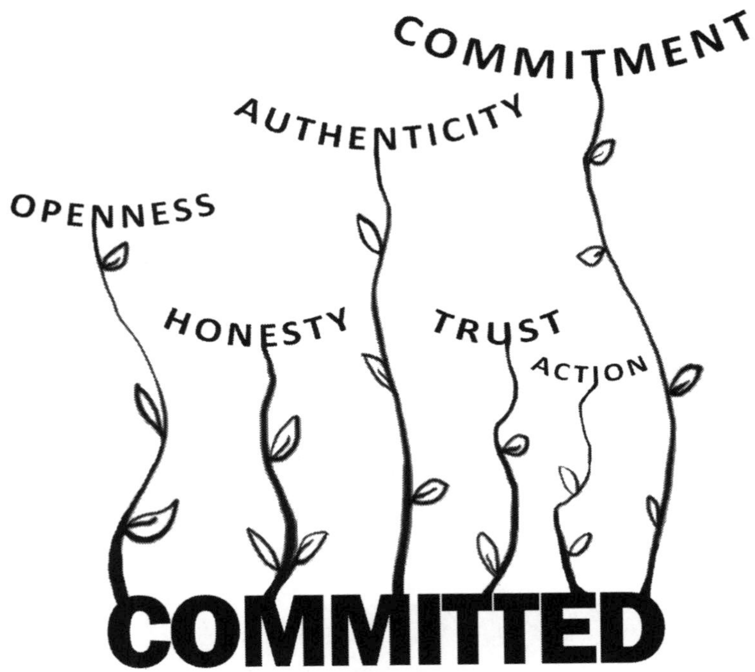

COMMITTED TO CREATE

1

Committed to Create

Those look like three strange words, right? And, yet they made such a powerful difference in my life and on the lives of those we work with that I wanted to share it here.

Speaking of difference, I hear so many people talk about "wanting to make a difference," which seems to be the latest "buzz" phrase. The reality is, you make a difference every day. You may want to ask yourself:

- What kind of a difference do you make?
- Are you living in a way or speaking in a way or developing relationships in such a way that you can make a difference and you will be heard?

Let me give you some history on how I learned about the phrase "Committed to Create" and what happened for me personally. As you read in the introduction, in 1996 I attended a four-day experiential training workshop that changed my life.

While I engaged in that workshop, I had the chance to divulge or declare the kind of person that I say I am, the kind of person I wanted to be, and to face my fears, my trepidations, and the realities of what blocked me from authentic relationships in my life.

More than once over the four days in 1996, I thought, "*This is a tough workshop! And one of my most amazing experiences ever."*

I found it amazing to be involved in a community, if you will, with about twenty-five or thirty other people and really have a chance to demonstrate through language and action; to be willing to face the truth about myself and to have a chance to engage in a relationship with people on a whole other level.

Most significantly, the workshop introduced me to something similar to the phrase "Committed to Create." Understand that phrase and you'll understand why I created Powerhouse Learning. I want to expand a little bit about why those three words are so powerful. It seems trite that such a simple phrase can make such an amazing impact in your life. I hope it catapults you into positive action the same way it motivated me all those years ago.

What Experience or Emotion Do You Want to Create?

The basic idea behind Committed to Create is: What experience or emotion do you want to evoke in the other party?

Truth time: You cause an experience or emotion every time you're involved with another human being.

How can you prepare? Peak performers and avid learners use mental rehearsal as one of their key skills. Elite athletes come to the field ready to play because they've played the game in their minds many times before they act. Playing out scenarios and making decisions beforehand, in your mind, will help you be better prepared when the time comes to move.

For example, every time I walk into a meeting either as a speaker or a participant, or speak with someone on the phone, I think in advance, "What am I **Committed to Create**?" It's usually best to use a one word answer.

My list often looks like this. I am Committed to Create:

- ✓ openness
- ✓ honesty
- ✓ authenticity
- ✓ trust
- ✓ action
- ✓ commitment
- ✓ etc.

Making a list of what I am Committed to Create prepares me to work on the core issues in order to make progress for me and for the other party. My list helps me help them achieve what they say they want.

Spoiler alert: Committed to Create is the BY WHEN, the action item, for this chapter.

Let me give you a concrete example of how Committed to Create shapes everyday behavior. Imagine you're a sales representative for your industry or a marketing representative (doesn't really matter which). Imagine you have customer contact daily both in person and over the phone, or you work in a call center or customer service or anything else. You're doing well, but not exceptionally well, and you can't figure out what blocks you from being great.

Picture the thoughts and emotions you have before you enter interaction with another human being. If your interactions with other human beings are large factors in your compensation, then each conversation could bring a lot of extra pressure, right?

In mapping out the conversation mentally beforehand, do you

prepare to engage the buyer or other person in a series of questions and dialogue in order to find out what is really important to them? OR do you worry too much about not making the sale, not being good enough, or whether this person will help you make rent? You also may be more focused on whether they will hound you about the results of the meeting.

Whether you think these thoughts consciously or not is irrelevant. Your mind is focused on you instead of the other party. In this case, I would say that you are Committed to Create a sense in the other person that you're distracted, that your questions mainly lead them to the decision that you only care about yourself, and you are more self-focused than being a good listener and a problem solver. Who wants to work with someone like that? Not me.

Here's an example of how to do this the wrong way: Suppose you've asked me to give a presentation to your group. Also assume for a moment that I'm a selfish narcissist and completely disinterested in you and your goals. In that scenario, I'm "Committed to Create" something —but instead of creating the positives I listed, I create a sense in all of you, an emotion or an experience that I'm a liar; that I'm dishonest. In this scenario your group has the emotion or experience that frankly, I've graced you with my presence today, that I'm better than you are, that I have all this knowledge, all of you are just little people, and I'm just here to make a buck. Consider that scenario. Surely you have encountered that experience if you've dealt with anyone outside your immediate coworkers. Or *maybe inside* your immediate coworkers!

By contrast, what if I'm "Committed to Create" openness, honesty, authenticity and bringing people closer together? What would I have to be willing to do or say in order to accomplish that?

What would my body language look like? How would I stand? How would I engage? I would convey an open attitude!

Stress and Bicycles!

Committed to Create.

These are powerful words and I want to caution you that you need to practice them where you have an opportunity to do so safely, possibly first with friends or family. You can be direct by simply saying to your associates, "Hey listen, I'm working on some new language or some new techniques and so I may fumble through it a little bit, so please be patient and give me honest feedback." If that is not an option, go into a situation, possibly in your call center or in a sales situation, embark on your next conversation with a client that you know and trust, and try it. Or, go into a brand new cold situation and try it and see what happens. Spend the time to be Committed to Create the positive impression in the life of the other person.

Why do I ask you to do this practice?

A friend told me a story that answers this question. My friend knows of a professional cyclist who, when not riding the roads, practices riding his mountain bike in his hometown. Every day my friend sees this cyclist riding with heavy saddlebags on either side of his bike. These saddlebags contain all his gear, energy drinks, and supplies that he needs when on the road in real-world conditions—rain, shine, steep hills and so on. Why does he weigh himself down when cycling close to home? Surely he doesn't need all that gear, right?

If the cyclist didn't practice with the saddlebags close to home and then tried riding with them up a steep hill in the mountains, his bike would wobble and throw him off balance—he could fall, or crash.

The same principle applies to practicing Committed to Create—before you venture out on the road and into a stressful encounter. If you try out these skills with the conversational equivalent of a leisurely bike ride, you won't wobble or crash when you try to use them when you have to fire someone or confront your spouse about the monthly budget.

I realize that even having to THINK about that exercise could bring on some stress and that brings me to my next point.

STRESS, in my opinion, has a lot to do with the way we choose to handle life's challenges. If you see circumstances and things that have happened as neutral, without emotion, and then look honestly at the emotion you label them with, this approach will help you feel as if you have more control over the way you handle the things in life that happen to you.

Exercise

Here's a guide and I'm going to use questions in succession to give you an example of what this can sound like. Begin by asking yourself:

> **"What are you Committed to Create? What's the experience or emotion you want to evoke in another party?"**
> **Answer:**_____

For example, let's just say your answer is: **Overcome a conflict or to deal with a difficult person.** If you're using one word like I've asked you to do, above, perhaps you say **reconciliation**.

If I have a conflict with another person and I want to break through that conflict and find reconciliation in the relationship. I would begin by asking questions like this:

- "I'm wondering…"
- "I've been thinking about…"
- "I've noticed that…"
- "What happened?"
- "What would you like to have happen?"
- "What would it take for you to…"
- "Are you willing?"
- "Are you open?"

Let me go through some of these and give you some scripts so you understand the context of what I'm referring to.

"I'm wondering if we could talk about something that's been bothering me lately?"

"I've been thinking about the conversation we had the other day and I noticed that you and I maybe aren't connecting well on this project?"

"Do you notice the same?"

"What happened?" or "Are you okay?"

"Are you having a tough time?"

"Is there anything that I can do to help you?"

"What would you like to accomplish on the project?"

"What would you like to have happen?" and "How can I help you get there?"

"What would it take in order for you to achieve what you said you wanted?"

"Are you *willing* to work on it together?"

"Are you *open* to you and I finding a way to fix it?"

Mediations

In fact, I've used those exact last two questions ("Are you willing?" "Are you open?"), among others, with individuals through formal mediation. Through this technique, I've been able to resolve difficult workplace conflict within two meetings. My predecessors in all of these mediations were unable to reach any movement in the prior six months. People sometimes wonder if I have a secret skeleton key to opening up these relationships. Once you understand and can deploy these tools including the skeleton key, you can have a lot of fun in helping others make difficult reconciliations.

Bottom line, I begin and end with questions about possibilities, not judgment. I say, "We judge ourselves by our intentions and everyone else by their actions." That's right, our perfect, wholesome angelic intentions. Well, maybe not so much!

A Gentle Warning

It would be foolish of me not to issue a warning here. The information, the principles, and the knowledge that I'm sharing with you have great power and you can use them for good or you can use them to manipulate for your own self-interest. I trust you to be wise. Please be careful how you use the information I bring you.

What I would like for you to do is take serious inventory about what's working in your life and what is not working in your life. Think about the relationships that you're engaged in now, whether at home, at work, your place of worship, it doesn't matter. Remember that we're all connected to human beings in one way or another. If on reflection you discover that you receive love and closeness, intimacy, and joy in your relationships, that's fantastic. The dynamic tool of Committed to Create and the other secrets could actually help further that cause and further your commitment to loving and caring about people. However, these techniques can also be used to coerce and manipulate.

Here's the problem with trying to use these tactics for nefarious purposes: people will feel something isn't right. You will cause a counterproductive experience or an emotion, including maybe one of confusion. A confused mind often says no.

I want to warn you to take a look in the mirror first before you engage. When you think about your relationships, think about what isn't working in your life and what you may have brought to those relationships to evoke the result that you have. Take a look at that first, and then be clear. You're unhappy somewhere in one of your personal relationships and it isn't working out for you. Further, you suspect you own a contribution to that situation in one way or another. What I'm going to ask you to do is to get clear on specifically HOW you've cosigned the negative result. Your part might reflect the choices you've made, the language you used, or your lack of willingness to keep your promises.

When you have clarity in your vision, next ask, "What am I Committed to Create? Am I Committed to Create more joy, intimacy, closeness, vulnerability, authenticity in my life?" Great! Use these tools that I bring you.

But if you only want to get something from someone, you may well indeed reach those goals at a cost. These are very, very powerful methods, but it's not going to work for you for the long haul.

When you use the power of Committed to Create, tap in to

make sure that your desire is not solely for your self-interest and your self-indulgence, but also for the other party.

Ask yourself:

- What is the result you're getting from the relationship?
- Is that relationship one of reciprocity?

If it's not, there's something missing that you have to face eventually.

And a Word from Terry Bradshaw

Terry Bradshaw. Most of you know who he is. He's hilarious, isn't he? He says, "Being gifted intellectually is only a small part of the equation of success. Concentrate on the factors you have the control over like persistence, self-discipline, and confidence. Far more failures are due to the lack of will than the lack of ability."

Your **BY WHEN**

Your official **BY WHEN** is to go into your next communication thinking about what you can do to set the tone based on your Committed to Create and take inventory on how the conversation went and if you noticed a difference in your results. What kind of changes can you make to get what you want out of life? See, you have the power within you to make these changes right now.

I'm looking forward to hearing your Committed to Create stories. Please log on to Powerhouselearning.com and send me a note to report back after you have tried this.

Takeaways

- "Committed to Create" is powerful.
- What are you Committed to Create?
- What experience or emotion do you want to evoke in the other party?
- You cause an experience or emotion every time you're involved with another human being.
- Mentally rehearse important interactions you have. Peak performers and avid learners use mental rehearsal as one of their key skills.
- Every time you have an interaction with another human being, think in advance, "What am I Committed to Create?" It's usually best to use a one word answer—for example, openness, authenticity, trust.
- If all your thoughts are about you, the other party will sense it and have an emotion or experience that you're all about yourself.
- If instead you want to bring people together, for example, your body language and words will reflect that.
- Try practicing with family members, friends, trusted associates or even in business calls. "I'm working on some new language or some new techniques and so I may fumble through it a little bit, so please be patient and give me honest feedback."
- Ask questions to break through a conflict and find reconciliation. Two key questions: "Are you *willing* to work on it together?" and "Are you *open* to you and I finding a way to fix it?"
- Be careful how you use Committed to Create—if you only

use it to get something from someone, it won't work for you in the long haul.

- Committed to Create can help further your commitment to loving and caring about people.
- Make sure when you use Committed to Create that your relationship is one of reciprocity and is also about the other party.
- Take a look in the mirror and take stock of what isn't working in your life—how have you helped create that negative result.

*What kind of changes can
you make to get what you
want out of life?*

THE EXECUTION OF CHOCOLATE CAKE

2

The Execution of Chocolate Cake Aka "What I Get"

In my experience, people really want to change. Most people do see the need for improvement or privately wish they had the ability to think or do things differently. Think about it: If people didn't want to change they wouldn't spend millions on diet programs and self-improvement material. As the weight loss ads say, results vary! Some people still can't lose weight and they wonder why the diet doesn't work—why nothing changes.

You may have heard the commonly held opinion that fear keeps us from change. Many programs begin from this assumption and focus on overcoming the fear as the primary pathway to change. I think the real impediment is something different entirely, something you might not expect.

Chocolate Cake

If you are a chocolate lover, you cannot resist chocolate cake. Impossible. A quick survey of the ingredients will reveal much to our consternation that chocolate cake is packed with items that are not good for your health. Your taste buds may love chocolate cake, but your body finds most of the things that make chocolate cake so delicious to be considerably toxic. Butter, refined sugar, food coloring, and many other components will make you sick if you eat it consistently. Additionally, the calories contained within even a modest slice rule out practically all other food items for a day's worth of recommended intake. If chocolate cake harms us, and we can pretty much agree it's not a health food, why is it that we continue to make and consume this product? Why do people continually devour items that will add inches to their waist and eventually ruin their health?

The reason that most us don't change is not that we fear changing or we can ignore our aversion to the negative aspects of our current behavior. Truth: We get something out of staying stuck. We enjoy an inherent reward to our inaction that is greater or more motivating than overcoming the fear and taking action. ***If the price we pay were compelling enough to make us change, no one would eat another piece of chocolate cake in their life. Ever.*** To put it another way, there's *nothing* good about chocolate cake; yet there is *everything* good about chocolate cake!

You can work on overcoming your specific fear for years, but contrary to what you have heard, the path to change begins elsewhere. *The single biggest impediment to change is the lack of appreciation and recognition of the reward you get from continuing to operate in the same manner.* You always reap some benefit from remaining stuck in the same patterns, behaviors, and consumption. The benefit is not immediately obvious, but in reality, even if the behavior harms you like chocolate cake, you receive a reward for continuing in the same fashion. The late Wayne Dyer once said that everything we do has a benefit.

To make real progress, you want to understand specifically the *benefit* you gain from your current conduct. I'm not talking about a calculated cost-benefit analysis, which doesn't work. If you've tried it you know this to be true.

I've used the chocolate cake concept over the years to help people make dramatic changes in their life. Don't be deceived by the relative simplicity of this approach. This ranks as one of the toughest assignments you'll ever complete if you are serious about changing your life.

Exercise

Create two columns and several rows on a sheet of paper. At the top center of your paper I want you to **write something you really want but haven't achieved yet**, or an obstacle to change you can't overcome. On the top left column, I want you to write, THE PRICE I PAY, and on top of the right column, WHAT I GET.

Let's start with the easy column: THE PRICE I PAY. For example, what price do you pay when you eat chocolate cake? Easy. It's full of calories, empty calories, with very little real nutritional value in chocolate cake. By the way, don't tell me about cake having milk, and eggs, and other "good" stuff…we all know better!

And now for the hard part: WHAT DO I GET? You get to eat chocolate cake! We love how it feels to indulge in a little piece of chocolate heaven. We love the taste, the texture, and how it makes us feel. That's what we GET. You can add your own twist on the above emotions, but suffice it to say, chocolate cake brings us temporary bliss.

Now the hard part: Is eating chocolate cake really worth it? Is the price you pay enough to make you swear off chocolate cake forever? In the traditional cost-benefit analysis, you would weigh the pros and cons of your actions. Even with all the cons clearly highlighted in front of you, you'll find it nearly impossible to resist this temptation. How many times have you stared down at the plate of silky goodness and despite your important diet goals, your firm resolution to be skinny, your solemn vow of caloric poverty, and said, "Forget my diet. I'm eating this cake anyway." You pay the price, again and again, despite your protestations and contrary desires.

So Obvious Sheldon Can't See It

Many of you know the hit TV series "The Big Bang Theory," with its indomitable lead Dr. Sheldon Cooper (Jim Parsons). Sheldon pontificates, lectures his friends, and drives them crazy with his habits. He pays the costs of social isolation and misunderstanding—a source of comic relief in the series. However, he gets to enjoy a sense of control and superiority over others, to self-obsess, to show off his intellect and to feel special. In the series, his friends and his committed relationship with Dr. Amy Farrah Fowler (Mayim Bialik) help humanize him.

A Clear Price

When I work with people who have asked me to help them make dramatic change happen, they are very clear about what they don't want in their life. They all cite what they don't want to do any longer, what they wish to overcome, and how they desire to be different. We all have something we wish to change, if we are honest.

You know what else people are very clear about? The price they pay. Most people see the obvious price tag for your behavior.

You can clearly delineate the negative aspects of your vice or habit: procrastination, smoking, weight loss, or not embracing success. You know the cost of your current position, starkly present and top of mind.

For example: What price do you pay for procrastination in your career or marriage? Inherently, you value time as a precious and quickly dissipating commodity. We only have so many years to become the person we wish to be, to grow at work or home. The people I help can clearly articulate the costs of continuing to put off taking the desired action.

What about lack of time management or efficiency? Easy. In an eight-hour workday, how much of your time counts as productive? You can chart, graph, and spreadsheet yourself into a finite and compelling pictogram of the precise amount of waste. You can specifically quantify the price you pay for this behavior. We have no illusions about the price of inefficiency.

How about smoking cigarettes, a particularly insidious habit? The price you pay for smoking is your life! The costs don't get more obvious or severe than that. We all know smoking causes cancer, emphysema and various other life-shortening effects. If this price was enough, and it's as high as it gets, people would stop smoking immediately once they learned of its deleterious consequences…clearly, people still smoke.

But what if you wrote your desired change as "to embrace success"? What price do you pay for NOT opening your arms to what the world has for you? Again, perhaps you can tell me what you must pay to continue to shirk from the challenges that bring success.

As you can see, the easy part is uncovering the price you pay for your present condition.

Now for the hard part: What do you GET out of it? What real benefit do you receive from staying stuck? There has to be a reward or prize for choosing to ignore your craving for change and continue along the path of mediocrity. If you didn't GET something out of your current behavior and the price you pay for it is obvious to you, you would have changed long ago.

To further illustrate the power of what you GET out of your current patterns, I want you to think about why people stay in abusive relationships. You may have experienced this person- ally or witnessed this phenomenon in your own family. If you've ever looked at a couple with this type of trouble and searched helplessly to understand how and why the victim cannot force herself/himself to leave, you will grasp the point I'm making here. Even in the most extreme circumstances with an exorbitant price, we continue to pay it because we GET something in return. Even when the thing we GET may cost our life! Even when someone endures reaffirmation of a negative belief, abuse or neglect, the payer stays in those situations we see as unfathomable because only the payer can truly uncover what they GET in return. Please note that I'm not saying this to blame the victims of domestic violence—especially since the most dangerous time, especially for women, is after victims leave their abusers. Further, there is no excuse for abuse. **<u>Period.</u>** I want to help people in this horrible situation move past their negative beliefs and make the call to the domestic violence hotline.

Many of you have heard, and it is true, that our mind is so powerful that it will not put you in a place where you're worse off than your current state.

The chocolate cake exercise is very difficult yet life-changing. I think it's one of the most powerful things I could ever share with you and I have seen people overcome amazing obstacles by going through this experience.

I'd like to share a story about one of my coaching clients who once sent me fourteen (!) pages of material on this PRICE vs. GET exercise. I found her answers very candid and authentic. You'll benefit from walking through this example as you start to incorporate this powerful tool into your work and or personal life. I'm including some of her entries:

At the top of her paper was a statement, "I WANT TO BE OTHER-FOCUSED."

PRICES:

I put people off.

I don't make my goals.

I sabotage my relationships.

I come across as a perception that I don't want something so I am misunderstood.

I'm not listening so I still I miss a lot.

It leads to distance in my relationships.

I'm lonely.

I'm confused.

I'm hurt and I'm angry.

She pays all those prices or not being more other-focused, in her own words. You can see toward the end how much it costs her emotionally to remain stuck. You may say, "Sheesh, why wouldn't she change?" It looks so obvious from outside. Rationally, we would think that the negative aspects, the price we pay for this behavior, would be enough to make anyone want to change. At this point, you need to dig deeper and figure out what my client

GETS from continuing unchanged. Let's take a look at what else she put down.

GETS:

I get to pontificate.

I get to explain myself.

I get to teach.

I get to be right.

I get to indulge in knowledge.

I get to appear important.

I use run-on sentences to get the satisfaction of explaining myself so I can feel justified in being right.

And I get the satisfaction of explaining myself so that people don't think I'm the one that's to blame.

At first it seemed that any one of the prices she paid—anger, loneliness, being misunderstood –would be enough to make someone desire change. However, unless we examine the payload inherent within that behavior, we will never fully understand the reason change has not already taken place. We will miss the very reason that she has remained unmovable.

The client and I discussed her responses at length. She made huge progress in completing the assignment. In addition to some of what I've shared here, it became obvious during our discussion that she also gets ramble on and feel as if she's sharing information and knowledge with people in her desire to feel important. She plays *not to lose* instead of playing to win. She plays it safe and gets to withhold. What she truly GETS is to avoid emotional investment, and it goes on and on in more detail.

I know the power of this work, and I also know most people

find it heavy at first. I promised you (and the client) that we would get down to core issues and difficult life challenges—this is one of them.

This exercise began with her clearly stated desire to be other-focused. After some digging, she as well as and you reading at home understand what PRICES she pays. If she stops there, change will continue to elude her. ***But if she focuses on what she's GETTING out of it, then that focus will compel her to change more than anything else!*** She will realize she's living in hypocrisy every time she indulges in the WHAT I GET. She will drift further away from what she really wants. Understanding WHAT I GET puts you on the real pathway to lasting change.

If you take nothing else away from this book, please revisit this exercise and incorporate it into your life.

Your BY WHEN

Do the PRICE I PAY vs. WHAT I GET exercise in this chapter. Write down what you really want for your life and then write down the PRICES YOU PAY for not moving in the direction of your dreams then what you GET out of staying stuck. Do the tough thing; do the exercise. It will be incredibly powerful, I promise.

> *"Up to a point a man's life is shaped by environment, heredity, and movements and changes in the world about him. Then there comes a time when it lies within his grasp to shape the clay of his life into the sort of thing he wishes to be. Only the weak blame parents, their race, their times, lack of good fortune, or the quirks of fate. Everyone has it within his power to say, 'This I am today; that I will be tomorrow.'"*
> —Louis L'Amour

<u>Takeaways</u>

- People really want to change.
- Most people think fear of change stops them.
- People don't change because they benefit from their behaviors—for example, eating chocolate cake.
- For most people the benefit of a behavior, such as eating chocolate cake, outweighs the price they pay.
- If the price of eating chocolate cake became too high for people and outweighed the benefits, people would stop being stuck.
- People are very clear about the prices they pay and what they don't want in their life. They don't know what they get from the behavior they want to change—for example, smoking; overeating; procrastination.
- The easy part: Uncovering the price you pay. The hard part: Dipping deeper and discovering what you get.
- Write down what you really want for your life and then write down the PRICES YOU PAY for not moving in the direction of your dreams then what you GET out of staying stuck.
- If you just focus on what PRICE you pay, change will continue to elude you.
- If you focus on what you're GETTING out of staying stuck – that focus will compel you to change more than anything else!

Up to a point a man's life is shaped by environment, heredity, and movements and changes in the world about him. Then there comes a time when it lies within his grasp to shape the clay of his life into the sort of thing he wishes to be. Only the weak blame parents, their race, their times, lack of good fortune, or the quirks of fate. Everyone has it within his power to say, 'This I am today; that I will be tomorrow.'

—Louis L'Amour

CONVERSATIONS
FOR ACTION

3

C4A Conversations For Action

Conversations for Action (C4A), an important foundational piece for this book, remains one of my greatest paradigms to transform communication from a concept into tangible Action that Drives Results. I know that helping someone move from dialogue to interpretation and bringing the recipient through to the desired result are not easy tasks.

The Conversations For Action tool forms the core of everything that I teach in my coaching and training practice, and it has helped transform the lives of thousands of individuals that I've worked with.

Because I've engaged in coaching, training, and educating for a long time, the cumulative experience has taught me a great deal about how people think, how they act, and what binds them together in relationship, as well as what separates them and pulls them apart.

C4A is about bringing conversation into being; using language not just for speaking but as a catalyst for doing.

Both People and Performance Oriented

This human technology is both people <u>and</u> performance oriented; one that produces immediate and long-term, continuing results. This method has been proven very effective in creating self-governing individuals.

Why This Process?

Our experience shows that the major impediment to achieving goals is not a lack of technology or strategic planning, but is found in the human element.

We believe that making and keeping agreements is the most effective way to pursue and achieve shared goals and visions. If used the way we instruct, our specialized C4A process will *dramatically improve the results in your company within 30 days.*

We have found that this methodology focuses the team on common areas and creates a quickened awareness and activity level towards positive change.

We have seen this topic literally transform the business culture and influence the personal lives of hundreds of individuals the first time they understand it! Best known for its ability to move your team from DISCUSSION into ACTION, we think you will be amazed at the dichotomy: **C4A seems so simple:** Promise; Commitment; Agreement; Request; and (my addition) BY WHEN. Yet you will find it intricate to learn because it will demand you be an Observer <u>and</u> a Participant as you implement its principles in your life and the lives of those you impact every day.

The foundation of this work began from Fernando Flores in

the 1970s. He shared that we all communicate in 5 ways: promises, requests, assessments, declarations and assertions.

C4A can be used as the beginning, middle and ending of everything we do in our interactions with others. It reveals character, strategic intent and action plans.

The power of the Conversations for Action framework is that it applies equally to people in all walks of life, different continents and cultures, and organizational roles. As I learned in my childhood travels and later in my coaching work, relationships with people remain the same no matter where you go. Whether you are in the boardroom or visiting family in another country, I want to help you develop better interactions, help you deal with difficult conversations as well as tough times, and help you move into action if you feel stuck.

I am known for giving very specific How-Tos. Here are the principles of Conversations for Action, this C4A as I call it:

- Promise
- Commitment
- Request
- Agreement
- and – BY WHEN

To master this technique, you'll need to understand each stage and how the situation naturally flows through this progression. Let's dive more deeply into each component.

1. Promise

We start with promise and commitment. In all these years of working in organizations, I find most people still cannot tell me the difference between a Promise and a Commitment. When I stand up in front of audiences and ask the audience randomly to give me those answers, I find many, many different things. People say, "Well, a promise is not as important as a commitment." Or "Commitment has more to do with your intent." "One is more serious than another." "One has a consequence, the other doesn't."

You see the problem. How can I expect to have great communication anywhere in my life, whether in business or my personal life, if I don't have a clear idea about what these words mean to me and to my department, my team, my family?

You may notice people don't use the word "promise" that much anymore. In fact, if someone told you, "Okay, I'll do it--I promise," you think of the used car salesperson that says, "Trust me."

Actions speak louder than words.

Simply put, a Promise (Step 1) encapsulates the **words** that you say and a Commitment (Step 2) involves the **actions** that you're willing to take, no matter what, in order to achieve or fulfill your promise. (In this section, I capitalize Promise to illustrate a point.)

Think about it: we give people our word in response to questions we receive multiple times a day:

"Hey! Give me a call."

"Let's get together sometime."

"Say 'hi' to your kids for me."

"Can you have that on my desk right away?"

"I'd really like to talk about our budget."

"Take the trash out, will ya, honey?"

We use and hear these (or similar) questions and statements all the time and yet they don't move us into action. Why? Look at how vague and ambiguous they sound. Yet they have become a part of our "norm"—the status quo that ultimately brings us a lot of disappointment.

Often-times when someone gives a promise (or at least we discern or think that they have given us a promise), two things happen:

1. We expect them to follow through.
2. We still fail to act and follow through if they don't do their part! In other words, someone says they'll do something and when they don't act, we don't act either.

Years ago, when two people shook hands, it was a way for one person to "give" their word, to give a part of themselves. If you'll notice, we still shake with our right hands, a symbol from a time when, by doing so, we left ourselves vulnerable without the protection of our sword. Thus, a handshake had tremendous trust and implied agreement built into the action. It also gave the recipient the right to claim the promise, and to call another out if they did not keep their word or their end of the contract. The other party gave implicit permission to do so! Yet now we make too many excuses, including my least favorite, "I'm so busy."

How many times have you made Promises today? This week? Little things and big things where you told another person you would do something, with and without a BY WHEN. And how many of those things did you complete when you said you would do them?

How many Promises have people given you? Even those you can think of that do and do not include deadlines? Do you remember any specificity—for example, "I'll make dinner for you Friday night"? If not, you'll find there is a less likely chance of things happening the way either party expected.

Broken Promises

Too many broken promises can damage relationships, ruin a corporate culture and breed distrust throughout your organization. However, when we have a Promise and a Commitment, we lay responsibility on the shoulders of the party that accepted this responsibility. Yet though we inherently know this is how the social contract works, often promises are broken.

When I give the other party my word, the recipient of the promise has the right to claim the promise. Don't they? If I say I'm going to meet you for dinner at seven and I just don't show up, you have the right to pick up the phone and say, "Hey, what happened? You were going to be here at seven for dinner!" While the consequence for this failure may be a lonely dinner, all broken promises carry consequences. When the promise broken differs from a dinner date, the consequences may not be as obvious or reported by the person who was left alone.

People ask me all the time, "What happens if a promise is broken?" Participants in my trainings can often accept the premise that promises have duties and expectations on both sides. They also can't immediately see what happens when promises are broken. The deeper problem is that broken promises weaken and sully your integrity, despite who you profess to be.

Here's a common example of how this works: Silvia tells Jeff she will meet him for lunch at the café at 1:00 pm. If Silvia doesn't show up at 1:00 pm without so much as a phone call or text to explain herself, Jeff may eat his meal, leave, and return to work or any other action to take the place of the broken promise. Silvia may not realize Jeff might worry about her: did she have a car accident? Some other calamity that prevented her from arriving?

Silvia may also not realize what Jeff did to accommodate the appointment with Silvia. Not knowing why Silvia missed their appointment causes much confusion for Jeff that he must resolve. Did something serious or life threatening happen or is Silvia just a flake? In the absence of information, Jeff will pick an explanation that suits him and move on. If he made an accommodation, he likely will be even more perturbed.

What happens when Silvia asks Jeff to meet her in the future? Jeff, even if he agrees, will probably have a different expectation of Silvia. He may half anticipate she won't show up. Jeff may consider her promise worthless and double-book just in case. Jeff may not consciously hold this attitude and belief, yet Jeff may just start disregarding Silvia entirely.

What type of relationship can Jeff and Silvia have after Silvia breaks her promise? Perhaps Jeff forgives Silvia and she promises not to repeat the behavior, but Jeff is likely to hold her promises in little regard. The human emotional element will always supersede the pragmatic purpose behind their relationship, be it family, business-related, or a friend. Also, in practical terms, for Jeff to be productive, his results will come from people, not things. Jeff must spend his time and energy with people who will fulfill their commitments if he wishes to be successful.

You know that breaking promises uses up your energy too. When you break a promise, you disconnect in that relationship and you will lose valuable time trying to reclaim the energy it took to make the connection in the first place! You may or may not succeed in repairing the bond. For relationships to be healthy, people have to speak up about broken promises (not always easy). If someone fails to honor a promise, you owe it to yourself to call the party out. If you make a promise, keep it. Stay diligent and you will have a lot less wasted time.

One of the last things I will ask you to do if somebody breaks a promise to you is simple: **FIND OUT WHY.** I ask you to be willing to care enough to find out why. Without accusation. Your opinion may change if the circumstances were completely out of the person's control. Catastrophe doesn't necessarily follow your schedule. Once you realize the other person couldn't warn you and that life happens, your feelings will soften. If you struggle to understand the situation, you can put the energy you would have spent distrusting the other person to better use.

If the promise-breaker is you, be willing to step up, apologize, and make it right and don't ever do it again.

Avoid repeat offenses. Breaking a promise one time certainly weakens your integrity, but what about the person who fails to live up to their word more than once? If you have a person like this in your life, you owe it to yourself to have a frank conversation. You probably get nervous just thinking about that exchange. Also, you may be tempted to jump past reason and start with accusations and anger. However, I would like you to consider the following ways to communicate instead:

Instead of thinking/saying:	Consider:
"You idiot!"	"Do you notice that…"
"You never keep your word. I can count on you not to come through for me."	"I've noticed that you promised 'x' and 'y' was delivered; what is wrong?"
"This is what we've seen all along."	"What happened?"
"Nothing will ever change."	"What got in the way?"
	"What's missing?"
	"What's stopping you…"

Below are some examples of helpful conversation starters:

"Brandie, do you notice that the past couple of meetings, even though we've talked about it, you've consistently been 15 minutes late?"

"Brandie, I've noticed that you promised X and Y was delivered. Are you okay? Because it's just not to your normal standard. What's stopping you from achieving what you said you wanted when we met two weeks ago?"

Be willing to engage in conversation with people and keep your dignity. Sometimes all of us deserve a little bit of grace. We all feel under pressure. We all face tough times. In that spirit, I'd like you to consider the merits of having these conversations to open up communication, reconciliation, and results.

Honor In An Unexpected Place

In popular culture, the only group that always succeeds in keeping promises and getting others to honor promises in return is the Mafia. I don't mean to imply that we should all live like characters in *The Godfather* or threaten violence. However, you have to admire the non-negotiable rules the Mafia live by. The consequences for violating those principles often go beyond a stern talking-to. If only we held society at large to a similar standard.

The stakes for breaking promises range in severity depending on the responsibility inherent in the profession. If your waiter breaks his promise, the consequence may be a cold meal or the wrong entrée. Not enjoyable, but certainly survivable.

If your promises involve heavy equipment, contractual risk transfer or any other area of commerce where injuries and property damage can be costly, your broken promises carry hefty penalties—and possibly legal trouble. Your lack of fulfillment may actually constitute a breach of duty, in which case you would be liable to pay for those damages.

More on the mobster movies. Most of them involve the same type of character so any one will do. Think of the lifestyle Don Corleone leads. The mob doesn't carry that lifestyle very long without making sure people hear and obey instructions. I suggest you become a bit more like Pesci or Don Corleone. Hold yourself and those who work for you to a high standard. Perhaps without the gruesome consequences, but you get the idea.

If the honor code works for La Cosa Nostra, there's no reason why civilians can't keep their promises as though their lives depend on it. Granted, maybe your broken promise won't cause you to sleep with the fishes, but how much more diligent would you be if you acted as if that were the case?

I'm obviously making an absurd metaphor. However, I would like to see this sort of diligence or honor code or Client Relationship Management in many other businesses. You know that we make a lot of promises to prospective customers, prospective business associates, friends and co-workers that we somehow don't find the time to keep. **Then we wonder why we need to worry so much about client retention... because perhaps our broken promises and our client woes are connected?**

Let's consider a non-fictional example of an industry that keeps promises or bad things happen and clients get upset: Attorneys. Lawyers get a bad rap in our society. We say, "Ah! Those lawyers, you know they rip people off. They take our money. They do all these kinds of things."

I hold a different view of attorneys because I had an experience years ago in which I needed to engage an attorney to help me with being reimbursed for tenants that had trashed my house. And I don't mean small, but over $20,000 worth of damage!

When you watch an attorney practice law you see the difference between the stereotype and the reality. Granted, when I observed my attorney in action, my funds and property being at stake ratcheted up my attention, yet even without that sharp focus I could see the truth: Attorneys deal with an absolute level of commitment.

In John Grisham's novel <u>The Client</u>, Mark Sway, who learns secrets that put his life in jeopardy, hires attorney Reggie Love for the princely sum of a dollar. Reggie fights to save Mark's life and commits completely to helping him even though she risks more than billable hours—she faces the same dangers as Mark and threats to her own law practice.

My attorney showed the same level of commitment as Reggie Love. When we had an agreement on the table, when all parties shared a handshake, when the other party gave verbal recognition and a verbal statement that showed the intent of fulfilling that statement through action, yet the person did not show up or do what they said they were going to do, my attorney jumped <u>right on it.</u> I know my attorney would do the same if I had broken my word. My attorney gave instructions with immediacy and attached specific consequences for non-compliance.

You may find, as I did, that when these professionals discharge their skills on your behalf, your attitude toward their methods changes quickly. *They understand the psychology of Promise and*

Commitment much more than many other business people that I work with.

A final example was a conversation I had with a friend named Greg many years ago when I was first learning about creating power over circumstances in order to keep my promises. He said, "After my breakthrough in this area I began to wonder what it would be like for me to be the kind of man that always kept my promises. To have that kind of integrity."

I thought it was a profound inquiry. So he lived his life to be clear and present at all times. If he could not make an appointment, he asked to reschedule but did not make it a habit. He was careful about the way he communicated with people; he didn't say things randomly and not imprint them and made sure he could fulfill what he said. To me, it was a great illustration of this principle and certainly the way I endeavor to live my life as well!

2. Commitment – The Daily Triumph of Integrity Over Skepticism

The next step beyond a Promise is a Commitment.

I have a customer in New York. When this customer started with me, I had a call with the office manager who was upset with the owner. She told me how happy she felt that he called me in to help with the office. And in very short order she told me how discouraged and disappointed she and the staff felt about the office.

Immediately I said, "Is it because leadership doesn't keep their promises?"

She replied, "Oh my God, how did you know?!"

No big surprise here. Skepticism, disappointment, and disillusionment are the symptoms of broken promises. Always.

In contrast, commitment means the willingness to have the integrity to pay the price to do whatever it takes to keep your word (barring any catastrophe that prevents you, which you of course communicate to the other party about.) Why? Because it changes the face of things. Doing whatever it takes to keep your word is moving from Discussion into Action. It PROVES you mean what you say, that you care enough, that you give a dang. (It is everything, in my opinion!) It brightens the place up, increases morale, and makes productivity soar. It heals broken relationships as well as mistrust in marriages, and allows humans to move forward again.

PROMISE: A declaration, written or verbal, made by one person to another, that binds the person who makes it either in honor, conscience, or law to do or forebear a certain act. It gives the one to whom it is made the right to expect or claim the performance or forbearance of the act specified. Honor, for example refers to the social realm – the realm of our reputation and our good name. We are bound to perform or forbear the promised act in order to maintain and enhance our reputation. Honor is the ledger that continually measures our reputation with people – when we keep or break our word, we either add or subtract from the ledger.

COMMITMENT: Commitment is what transforms a promise into reality; it is the words that speak boldly of your intentions, and the actions that speak louder than words. Commitment is the stuff character is made of; the power to change the face of things, it is the daily triumph of integrity over skepticism. Commitment shares the same root in Latin as promise – to send with. Commitment is the strength of character to go the second mile, or the third, or the fourth, whatever it takes to keep our promise. Commitment is the determination of the will that is *sent* with a promise.

The prices we pay to keep the promises we make reveal the commitment motivating us.

"There are only two options regarding commitment. You're either in or out. There's no such thing as a life in-between."
—*Pat Riley*

Commitment fuels the third step, the Request.

3. Power of a Request

Let's assume you have a complaint. Things seem strained in your relationships. When you make plans, the other party rarely comes through.

Consider using the POWER OF A REQUEST. A request moves people from complaining about something into taking action. Many studies in management reveal what employees esteem to be important and what some of their greatest complaints are in the workplace. One of the things at the very top of the list of all complaints is the temperature in the office!

If you work in a large corporate environment, you encounter two factions: those who enjoy the frigid tundra and those who secretly wish their cube sat on the surface of the sun. Interestingly, people seldom fall somewhere in the middle—and those people don't complain; they just bring sweaters.

In most office buildings, the debate usually rages on for years. Sally turns the A/C down secretly on her lunch break. Joe comes back from lunch and notices that he starts to sweat in two seconds, so he resets the thermostat to the North Pole setting. The game continues and neither party wins. The entire office sees Sally wearing a parka at her desk in the middle of July and Joe dripping sweat throughout the office in the afternoon. If you looked up passive-aggressive in the dictionary, you'd see pictures of Joe and Sally next to the definition.

Using the POWER OF A REQUEST will interrupt the pattern of passive-aggressive insurrection and establish a truce once and for all in the hot-versus-cold wars.

Let's say Joe says, "Hey, Sally! Are you the one in charge of the temperature? Would you be willing to turn it down a couple notches?" This is an effective and direct way to move people into action instead of listening to or making constant complaints, and then complaining maybe about the way things were handled.

Think about using the POWER OF A REQUEST when you feel frustrated, when you feel disheartened, when you're discouraged, and that request will at least let you know where you stand.

Three Answers to a Request

There are only three ways to respond when someone makes a request: YES, NO, or MAYBE (we negotiate). Nothing earth-shattering here. The important part for our purposes is to under-stand which response we truly receive.

An Italian friend of mine gave me a response to this question that I still find helpful to this day: "Well actually, the way I was raised was **no meant maybe** and **maybe meant yes** and **yes, well, you just want to make sure what that really means.**" Having been raised with little specificity benefited her in later years. As a reac-tion to the lack of certainty in her early life, she moved people into getting clear specific answers as a result.

I'll follow up my friend's quote with one of those Brandie sayings: **"We've been conditioned to accept philosophy without action as innovation."**

We see it in our media. We see it with politicians. We see it with some instructors and speakers and teachers. I call that RAH RAH.

You know what I mean. You feel the "RAH RAH" effect after a seminar, a podcast, or a training, when we go back to wherever we're going back to. Whether it's back to home or back to the office, we try to implement the things that the experts and teachers present in such a way that everything sounds so simple or so easy or so fantastic. We find that we are left in a world of disappointment and I'm going to tell you why that happens.

One reason: Adults and kids learn differently. Children sit in a classroom and they watch a teacher on the whiteboard or the blackboard, and they interact, maybe even through computer study, and then they come home and they do some homework, but they learn mostly through sitting at that desk, going through that process.

Adults learn through what we call experiential training, learning and imprinting—or learning by doing. Through implementation and practice the concepts start to take hold in the adult mind. When you listen to speakers or politicians it is not obvious at first glance that they have practiced many hundreds of hours to sound polished, and spent hours in salons or tanning beds to look good. It seems very natural. They have achieved success because they have used those methods in their own personal lives. When they stand up and they impart that information to you, the relative ease with which they deliver the information is deceptively simple. It takes lots of follow-up and hours of implementation to make change look effortless. The reality could not be more different!

Perhaps you've shared a motivational piece from one of these seminars with your team and you watch as the excitement builds, only to watch it fizzle shortly thereafter. Your team doesn't follow up. You get downhearted and don't follow up, either. It's why leaders become discouraged at the lack of results and it's why we don't continue to learn, grow and change at the pace that we would like.

FIRST, we think change is that easy, and SECOND, we think that we can tell someone what to do and then they will get it done. And how are they going to get it done?

GO AHEAD! ASK YOUR KIDS TO CLEAN THEIR ROOM

As children, our parents asked us kids to clean our room. I'll bet a tidy sum you were on the receiving end of this request, probably more than once.

Our Timeline or Theirs

When our parents issued this request, did they expect it to be done on their timeline or our timeline? They were not asking us to clean our room next week, month, or year. We knew they expected things to get done on their timeline, as in *now*. (Bonus points for saying "NOW" in that Mom voice.)

Kids have an entirely different sense of time and urgency than do parents. At a younger age, weeks seemed to last forever, and now that I'm over forty, months fly by faster than I'm comfortable recognizing. Einstein talked about relativity and the experience of time passing differently. Einstein must have observed kids and parents as well as physics.

From a parent's perspective, there was a request. Okay, okay, a demand. As kids, we didn't always see it the same way. What usually happened? Neither of us was happy. Mom followed "requests" with threats and potential repercussions: no TV, no cell phone and no Internet, perhaps.

Assuming we kids got away from video games and iPads long enough to clean our room, what type of job did Mom expect? Likely the spot check with white cotton gloves searching for the faintest of dust specks.

Our Standard or Theirs

When we were told something by our parents, did they expect it to be done to their standard or our standard? In our eyes, a smaller mountain of dirty clothes in the middle of the floor or under the bed indicates a cleaning job well done. We know what their standard looked like: no debris/dirty socks on the floor, orderly, free of odors and insects. They expected the work be done to their standard and usually become disappointed when they walked past our room only to see a slightly less disorganized HAZMAT zone.

Ad Infinitum—Ad Insanity

Then lastly, our parents often infused their request with another expectation. They made assumptions that having instructed the children to clean their room this time, they will make the connection that cleaning is now a regular function that they are expected to perform forever. Parents don't expect to have to issue this request a second time. From experience as a parent, I will tell you that this doesn't happen! Einstein said the definition of insanity is doing things the same way every time and expecting different results. Yet we make the same requests in the same way and expect change, ad infinitum, ad insanity.

These inherent assumptions built into our requests cause a lot of the disappointment in both in our personal and business lives. When we issue a request, we must consider our implied expectations, the standards and timeline that we expect, and whether or not the recipient shares those values and definitions. When in doubt, make certain. And beware the "TELL/DO" Method when you move to the next step after your request.

4. Agreement

The next step, once you make a request, is to get an agreement.

Tell/Do Method Does Not Work

The "TELL/DO" method does not work. It doesn't work with our children and personal relationships and it does not work in our business relationships. It's not enough to TELL someone to DO something and expect magic results. So I've come up with the method of AGREEMENT.

Here are examples in the real world of "TELL/DO" vs. AGREEMENT. I've used some of these examples in a business context because many of us are engaged in some sort of business capacity in one way or another. We interact with people and we trade information back and forth in one way or another. The AGREEMENTS have multiple steps and multiple suggestions to prompt the other party to engage. It takes more effort than the TELL/DO method but it's so worthwhile!

TELL DO	AGREEMENT
"Let me know if you have suggestions on what I've proposed."	"Will you agree your feedback is valuable to the project?" "BY WHEN would you like to get me your thoughts?"
"As a result/based on the information of/from our x (results), we have decided to implement the following changes…"	"Here are the results. Based on our vision for creating a more profitable/productive environment, we'd like your feedback on changes needed by (get or give a time). Then what is your department going to do differently and how will we know if you're on track?"
"You have 30 days to demonstrate…"	"We have met and discussed some changes that need to occur in line with our vision for the organization and things to make the department/position more efficient. I'd like to set up a 30-day plan for measurable improvement. What do you think/how do you feel about that? Does it make sense to you based on our discussions? What do you think needs to be done? If you were me, what would you suggest?"
"I've told them a hundred times, so this time I'm going to make sure they know that if they don't do X …" OR "I'm going to tell them to get on board, that they need to buy in…"	"Okay, as you know, we have a commitment or goal or objective this year to produce X." OR "How many of you /can you tell me what our goal is for this year/quarter, etc.?" "Okay, it is X." "So based on that goal, what are some of the creative ways you can think of to generate that result?" "Each of you send me an e-mail or bring your ideas to the next meeting, etc… and we will put together the 'BY WHENS.'"
"We've heard this all before; why don't we just give stronger/better deadlines?!"	"I'd like to see X result, how can we get other people involved? Who are the power players? How can we: (1) hear, (2) implement, and (3) measure if we're on track "

If you feel that you keep telling people what to do again and again and again, it is likely you do not have agreement. Such a simple word with a very powerful action connected. In fact, I say,

"WHEN WE HAVE AGREEMENT, WE HAVE ACCOUNTABILITY!"

What agreement do you have? How can your Conversations For Action (C4A) create agreement? How can they lead to BY WHEN, the final step?

5. BY WHEN

Here we come to the title of this book and the reason for its existence, or as the French might say, its *raison d'être*.

I use these two words. "BY WHEN" as my two favorite words in the English language, because using them transforms Promise into Commitment with significant awareness.

So if my attorney says to the other party across the table, "I need your answer by three p.m. today," my attorney uses a BY WHEN.

The anatomy of a BY WHEN looks like this:

Specific action + specific time and date = BY WHEN.

In contrast, BY WHENS that lack specificity sound like this: "Hey! Let's work on that in the next couple weeks" (elements of TELL/DO) or "Why don't you get back to me?" The problem with issuing a BY WHEN without commitment is that nobody knows where they stand. In fact, you don't even know where you stand on your own.

However, if I say, "Give me a call," a client might say, "Great! When are you going to call me?" (Commitment/Request) Or he/she might break out their calendar and start to make an entry. Perhaps he says, "How about Thursday at 9 a.m.?" (Commitment/Request).

If the client starts to suggest a time, my brain orients in a completely different direction. I calibrate my brain to focus on what my client is saying and I also pay attention to myself. All because my client uses the tool of BY WHEN—perhaps without even realizing it!

I agree to Thursday at 9 a.m. (Agreement). The BY WHEN cements the agreement.

"BY WHEN" is one of the most powerful things that I use to transform Discussion into Action.

In this example, if I say, "Call me by Thursday," there's no understanding, I am setting myself for likely disappointment. But if I say, "By Thursday at nine," you know it's by 9 a.m., or if I say, "Thursday by 5:00," you know it's no later than 5:00 p.m. Now, all the client and I need is to determine which Thursday we'll have our phone call!

However, if we follow the five steps of C4A, the decision about which Thursday we will have our call seems simple!

BY WHEN cements all the other steps as well.

Brandie tip: When working on projects without defined timelines or material that needs to be delivered from one party to another, use, for example, "by noon" or "by 5:00." Something like this: "Thanks for your order, Mr. Customer. In order for us to move forward, do you think you could send your final material Thursday by noon/by 5:00?"

In addition, if you are in the profession to use the phone frequently, make sure you end every call with an action, whether it be a timeline or whether it be to set another phone call. If it is a phone call, always know who will call whom. This simple little thing makes a BIG difference in your productivity.

Your **BY WHEN (HOMEWORK)**

#1: Think about promises that you have made and not kept in your life. How many can you list? Probably a lot if you're like me.

#2: Think of the promises made to you that have been broken. I've got a lot of those too.

What can you do to make sure that you're listening to the words you say and creating more agreements to avoid some of the disappointment through broken promise?

And can you live in such a way that you will keep all of your promises. And if so, how could that happen?

How can you help more people along their journey in life by being the kind of person to do what you say you will do EVERY TIME?

Takeaways

- Conversations For Action (C4A) uses the following steps: 1. Promise; 2. Commitment; 3. Request; 4. Agreement; and 5. BY WHEN

- Most people don't know the difference between a Promise and a Commitment.

- Promises are empty in our minds because people easily break them.

- Actions speak louder than words.

- A Promise (Step 1) encapsulates the **words** that you say and a Commitment (Step 2) involves the **actions** that you're willing to take, no matter what, in order to achieve or fulfill your promise.

- We give our word to people and vice versa several times a day, yet we/they don't always follow through.

- When someone gives us a promise, we expect him/her to

follow through, but if he/she doesn't act, we don't act either.

- How many Promises have people given you today? How many have you given? How many of those have been kept on either side?
- If you fail to show up for an appointment without an explanation, you have to spend energy mending the relationship.
- Broken promises damage relationships.
- If somebody breaks a promise to you, **FIND OUT WHY.** Be willing to care enough to find out why. Without accusation.
- Your opinion may change if the circumstances were completely out of the person's control. Disaster doesn't happen on your time schedule.
- If the promise-breaker is you, be willing to step up, apologize, and make it right and don't ever do it again.
- If someone breaks a promise, communicate without accusation with phrases such as "I've noticed that you promised 'x' and 'y' was delivered; what is wrong?" "What happened?" "What got in the way?"
- Mobsters and attorneys always enforce promises.
- Skepticism, disappointment, and disillusionment are the symptoms of broken promises. Always.
- Use Commitment (Step 2) to go beyond a promise.
- Commitment means the willingness to have the integrity to pay the price to do whatever it takes to keep your word (barring any catastrophe that prevents you, which you of course communicate to the other party about.)
- Doing whatever it takes to keep your word is moving from Discussion into Action. It PROVES you mean what you say, that you care enough, that you give a dang
- Commitment heals broken relationships, mistrust in

marriages, and allows humans to move forward again.

- Commitment is the daily triumph of integrity over skepticism.
- If you have a complaint, consider using the POWER OF A REQUEST (Step 3).
- There are only three ways to respond when someone makes a request: YES, NO, or MAYBE (we negotiate).
- Beware the "RAH RAH" effect—inspiring words but nothing happens.
- The Tell/Do method doesn't work. FIRST, we think change is that easy, and SECOND, we think that we can tell someone what to do and then they will get it done. And how are they going to get it done?
- If you think the Tell/Do method works, ask your kids (if you have them) to clean their room—or remember when your parents asked you.
- Do we expect it to be done to their standard or our standard? They may not be the same.
- You can repeat the Tell/Do method forever with no progress.
- Instead of Tell/Do after a request, use Agreement (Step 4).
- The next step, once you make a request, is to get an agreement all parties understand.
- When we have agreement, we have accountability.
- The final step in Conversations For Action is BY WHEN (Step 5).
- BY WHEN transforms Promise into Commitment with significant awareness.
- The anatomy of a BY WHEN looks like this: Specific action + specific time and date = BY WHEN. For example, "Please call me Thursday at 9 a.m."
- By When cements the Agreement (Step 4) and all the other steps.

Attitudes First

Behavior Second

4

Attitudes First, Behavior Second

Attitudes must come first, and then behavior second. Oftentimes when things are not working well in our relationships, whether it is at work or in our personal lives, we want to look at the behavior and address the behavior.

Let's move beyond behavior (action) to attitude. I've found that attitude is the posture of your heart and your mind in relation to that which you aspire or the other person aspires. Attitude determines our thoughts, our language—and the **why** behind our actions. We are wired to do things a certain way—sometimes without conscious thought! Once you uncover more of the reasons **why** you have continued doing the same things repeatedly, you can engage in a plan to break through it – and you will see an immediate result in the physical universe.

In the memoir and movie The Glass Castle, Jeannette Walls' alcoholic father Rex and her mother Rose Mary move the family from place to place, impulsively. The Walls children endure poverty, homelessness and rootlessness. Rex gives many explanations for this upbringing—he's unconventional, he marches to his own drummer, he wants his children to experience life outside what he sees as society's rules—but his children suffer and never achieve the happiness Rex promises. The movie is difficult to watch and you wonder about the real reasons why Rex repeats his mistakes even when his approach doesn't work.

When you act and as a result things don't work out, look at the posture of your heart, your intent. Your attitude. Your emotions. And then you can focus on the behavior, whether you're engaged in leadership or if you're a parent working with your kids. First, focus less on the behavior and more on what's going on underneath it, and you'll get a lot further.

Earlier, I mentioned a little bit about how we are wired underneath. At our core we have beliefs that we have developed over time. They came from our life experiences, our personal faith, and even through the experiences of others. I learned this principle many, many years ago.

At the very core of all of us rest our belief systems, or the things that we hold dear to us, even if they're unhealthy. The next thing is our emotions, or how we relate to the thing that we believe in. Next comes our thoughts about the matter, and lastly our behavior, sculpted by beliefs, emotions and thoughts.

What I'm asking you to do is examine your beliefs and how you relate or feel about them and then your actions or behavior that naturally follows.

One of the teaching stories I often tell is a **fictional** account about my distain for Cocker Spaniels. Full disclosure, I love animals, but you'll see why this is illustrative in a moment.

I say to people, "Imagine the following story." As a little girl I went across the street to visit my friend who owned a Cocker Spaniel. He wagged his tail and seemed friendly at first, but when I walked in the door to see my friend, that Cocker Spaniel looked at me sideways. Perhaps you've seen the look a dog gets before he attacks? It's as if you can see the thought bubble above his head, "Yeah, I'm going to bite this person." I started to walk past him and as soon as I did, the sucker nipped me on the ankle. Ouch!

How would you respond emotionally in the same situation? Initially, you don't think much about the emotions involved. If an animal has ever bitten you, you know the first emotion is SHOCK. Really? Did that just happen? Then probably fear and anger and distrust all at the same time. As a small child, I instinctively moved away from it – and fast! Understanding how I responded emotionally after this experience often takes years to fully appreciate.

Fast-forward years later in this imaginary example. I was in high school and I was dating this cute guy. He invited me over to do homework after school and meet his parents and have dinner. I felt jazzed, completely thrilled with the invitation and the possibilities, until I walked in the door. What type of dog did he have? You guessed it, a Cocker Spaniel! No stopping that wave of emotion and painful memory that hit me immediately. Avoidance, fear, freaking out – all at once. Then of course the feeling that I'm doing this in front of other people, including the cute guy, and they don't have a clue why I'm acting so weird.

It's easy to say in my imaginary scenario, "I can hold on to my aversion because that OTHER dog bit me years ago." As an adult, whenever I see a Cocker Spaniel, I immediately can choose an emotional response based on an event that happened decades before. That emotional response is important to evaluate simply because it shapes my behavior.

If you know anything about animals and bringing energy into a situation, horses, dogs, anything like that in real life, you actually end up *manifesting what you don't want*! In fact, it's very likely that if my date's dog had any tendency towards biting, then it will probably bite me because of my reaction and nervous energy. If that had happened, I and perhaps you would immediately blame it on the dog. That's natural–but it's not the whole picture. Many people would react and defend the dog. As an animal lover, I understand this!

Often, we go through life unaware of our attitudes and emotions and how they drive our behavior. When I see a Cocker Spaniel in my scenario, I don't rationalize through my prior experience and try to make sense of why I'm reacting—I just react. Breaking this chain and reshaping behavior is possible if you start with the "why" and understand the context. Simply asking the person to explain their behavior or assigning reasoning behind it without an appreciation for the **why** will leave both parties unfulfilled. We have to start by taking inventory. Then when we see a Cocker Spaniel, we can make a change. We can say, "Nice doggie," and mean it.

Your BY WHEN

I want you to write down some attitudes that drive the behavior you wish to change. For now, let's just make a simple list and write them down as they come to mind.

Takeaways

- Attitudes come before behavior.
- Attitudes/beliefs and emotions drive behavior.
- Attitude determines our thoughts, our language—and the **why** behind our actions.
- When you act and as a result things don't work out, look at

the posture of your heart, your intent. Then you can focus on the behavior.

- At our core we have beliefs that we have developed over time.
- At the very core of all of us rest our belief systems, or the things that we hold dear to us, even if they're unhealthy.
- Examine your beliefs and how you relate or feel about them and then your actions or behavior that naturally follows.
- If you fear something because of an event in your past, you bring that energy into the situation and the experience may repeat.
- Understand that you often choose an emotional response based on an event that happened decades before. That emotional response is important to evaluate simply because it shapes your behavior.
- Often we go through life unaware of our attitudes, beliefs, emotions and thoughts and how they drive our behavior.
- Breaking old patterns is possible if you start with the "why" and understand the context.
- You'll be more satisfied if you appreciate the "why" behind someone's behavior—and so will they.
- Take inventory of your attitudes and work backward to change your behavior.

TAKING
INVENTORY ☑

Taking Inventory

Taking inventory is a fact-finding and fact-facing process. One object is to uncover damaged and unsaleable goods. If the owner of a business expects to succeed, he/she must take regular inventory and discover the truth about the stock in trade. Hanging on to expired product or out of date fashions won't propel the store forward. As individuals, we can apply the exact same examination to our beliefs, attitudes, thoughts and behaviors.

I'm going to ask you to look at what kind of things you're avoiding—changing a job, having a difficult conversation—and what kind of things, such as fear and anxiety, are stopping you from getting what you want in life? You know from Chapter 4 that our attitudes, internal beliefs and emotions toward a certain thing or circumstance drive our behavior. All of us think, act and communicate from the inside out.

Some of you may say, "That's not necessarily true, Brandie, I react based on how people are around me or how circumstances play out."

I challenge that assertion because we have the ability and the control within all of us to determine how we will react to circumstances. If someone cuts you off in traffic, you choose your response to that event. You may choose expletives, hand signals, or ignoring the behavior. It may seem like a reaction without much thought or effort. However, if you had zero control over your reactions, the jails and prisons would be overflowing with commuters and other motorists across the country!

At your next opportunity, examine those "reactionary" behaviors. After the dust has settled, that is the time to attempt to understand what took place and how you can begin to change going forward. That is the time to take inventory—before you face pressure.

Who you are under pressure is the REAL you.

Take notice the next time you face a tough, high-pressure situation. Look deeply at your reaction after you receive some bad news, someone takes advantage of you or your family in some way, or a person at the office really gets under your skin. When you feel really upset, pissed off, or hurt is the time to look at whether you have IT (the reaction) or IT has you!

Exercise

Put pen to paper. Sketch out the situation, the circumstances, and the result. Try to walk back through your own beliefs and attitudes toward the situation and uncover what lies behind your behavior.

If a certain person really gets under your skin, what is it about them or the way they behave that causes you to react? Why do you have that reaction? What beliefs drive your attitude? You may say, "This person is arrogant, and I hate arrogant people." Okay, what is it about that characteristic you find objectionable? Did you have experiences in the past with strong personalities that convinced you to react in a certain way?

Be a Detective

Bad news or perceived attacks on loved ones are never welcome. If you've ever received bad news that involves others equally, you might be shocked to see different reactions. For example, if you have siblings and a relative becomes ill, or there is a death in the family, your siblings may react differently than you in response to the same stimulus.

It is not necessarily the outside events that control the behavior, but the inner beliefs and attitudes that shape what behavior we put on public display. You can easily misunderstand people in these situations because their behavior may not reflect the inner reality—but you can pick up clues. Interestingly, detectives watch the behaviors of suspects in order to find the individuals' motives and determine if the persons may or may not be involved in a crime. You can act as a detective and observe your own behavior, which—you guessed it—starts with working backward from your attitudes and beliefs. To paraphrase Sherlock Holmes, you can observe as well as see. Then take inventory.

If you take stock of your beliefs during life's challenges, you will better understand the sources of anxiety and the root causes behind your behavior. By understanding yourself, you can begin getting what you may really want out of life. If you can identify your driving factors you can overcome them.

I have overcome my deep drives, very difficult belief systems, childhood challenges, and my own twisted self-perception.

You can succeed, too. You can identify the things that are

stopping you and then you can do something about it. Here is the part where I say BY WHEN.

Your BY WHEN

Don't put it off or say maybe someday. Do the exercise. Write down what you want to overcome, your BY WHEN, and post it in your calendar, on your wall, or in your wallet.

Takeaways

- Every business needs to take honest, objective inventory. You can take inventory of your life.
- Look at what kind of things you're avoiding—changing a job, having a difficult conversation.
- Look at what kind of things, such as fear and anxiety, are stopping you from getting what you want in life.
- Circumstances do not dictate your life. If someone cuts you off in traffic, you choose your response to that event.
- Who you are under pressure is the real you.
- Take inventory of your attitudes and beliefs before you face pressure.
- Take notice the next time you receive some bad news, someone takes advantage of you or your family in some way, or a person at the office really gets under your skin.
- When you feel really upset, pissed off, or hurt is the time to look at whether you have IT (the reaction) or IT has you!
- Be a detective and observe your own behavior.
- Work backward from your attitudes and beliefs to find your true motives. Then take inventory.

- If you take stock of your beliefs during life's challenges, you will better understand the sources of anxiety and the root causes behind your behavior
- Understand yourself and overcome your driving factors to get what you really want.

PERSPECTIVE MATTERS

6

Perspective Matters

Near where I used to live in Idaho, we enjoyed pointing out to visitors an impressive deep canyon. Most of you know it as the place where Evil Knievel tried to jump the Snake River in 1974. Less than two miles away from the launch point flow the beautiful Shoshone Falls, a massive drop-off point in the middle of a vast desert.

When you first observe the landscape it appears barren and lifeless until you come upon this majestic wall of water plummeting over a cliff higher than Niagara. Stunning. Based on the time of year that you visit, you can enjoy a different view of Shoshone Falls.

In spring, the falls become mighty and vast. The runoff comes down from the mountains compared to late winter when the runoff drops to less than thirty percent of the levels eight months before. The melting snow and rising temperature melt the snowpack and the falls come alive.

By contrast, if you visit during the winter months, the falls seem much less impressive. You may wonder what all the fuss is about. The raging waterfall pictured in the brochure may appear nothing more than a trickle. When you add cold weather and possibly lack of sunshine, the very same place you imagined as magical looks common or at best marginally impressive.

Experience teaches us that things can appear differently depending on where, when, and how we see them. If we have faced adversity and overcome it, we begin to realize that situations do get better; things will change. Think of the anti-bullying campaign "It Gets Better." Rarely do people face insurmountable problems. One need only look to social media to see plenty of examples of people who were dealt difficult cards only to smile back at life.

An even more important lesson on experience and perspective comes after you have tasted success. How you respond or behave when you get a raise, the corner office or accolades reflects your inner attitudes and beliefs. Experience also teaches us that this too may be temporary. Many of the most successful people in life have experienced both sides, many times.

My challenge to you is to analyze how experience has changed your beliefs over time. What has influenced the change in your understanding of something you may have seen differently long ago? Perhaps you better understand the veteran fellow employee who seemed so salty and gruff when you first started working together now that you have spent ten, fifteen or twenty years working in the same industry.

Here comes my favorite part…

Your BY WHEN

- Write down your beliefs about a circumstance or situation. Pick intervals in your life:
- What did you think about this circumstance five years ago?

- How did you feel about it ten years ago?
- How do you feel now?
- Write down how your beliefs have changed over time. You'll be surprised how easy it is to accomplish when you have your BY WHEN.

Takeaways

- Experience teaches us that things can appear differently depending on where, when, and how we see them.
- If we have faced adversity, situations do get better, and things will change.
- How you respond or behave when you enjoy success reflects your inner attitudes and beliefs.
- Success may be temporary. So may adversity. Successful people have experienced both sides, many times.
- Analyze how experience has changed your beliefs over time.

It's not always about you

7

It's Not Always About You

Christopher Gardner, Jr: What are you doing?
Christopher Gardner: Paying a parking ticket.
Christopher Gardner, Jr:...But we don't have a car anymore.
Christopher Gardner: Yeah, I know...
—From *The Pursuit of Happyness* (2006) Quotes courtesy of IMDB.com.

People have their own issues to work through and their own challenges in life. Now some of you may say, "Of course, Brandie, we learned that in third grade!" However, we often forget all those life lessons from childhood. I would like you to remember that there are people that may be going through tough times at home or tough times in their business.

Maybe the people you deal with got some really bad news recently and they don't feel a need to share it with you. If you knew more about what people were going through, would you have a little more grace or forgiveness? Would you treat them with respect?

Years ago, I watched the movie *The Pursuit of Happyness* starring Will Smith. The movie is based on the true story of Chris

Gardner, who became a single father in 1981, and shortly after the separation with his wife, ended up homeless through real-life circumstances. The movie captivates us because any one of us could become homeless--these circumstances or chain of events are not outside the realm of possibility.

If all the dominoes came crashing down, where would I stand? That question kept running through my mind as the tale unfolded.

Regardless of each successive difficulty Will Smith's character, Chris Gardner kept showing up for work. He kept focused. He kept doing whatever it took for him to achieve what he said he wanted, with **no guarantee of a positive outcome** - quite the contrary. Each successive effort seemed to be met with yet more disappointment. After six months of dutiful work Chris Gardner had no job certainty. Regardless, he remained diligent and faithful.

In one specific scene, one of the board members at his company casually asked Smith's character to borrow five dollars. Routinely in offices, people ask for small favors and with few exceptions, coworkers are happy to lend such a small sum, most of which have also been on the receiving end. In the movie, the audience understands that this is Chris Gardner's **last five dollars**; worse, he literally has *no more money* for any of his needs. Faced with these circumstances, Chris Gardner simply gave the board member the money, having faith that it would work out.

How often do we walk through life, clueless about those around us?

This simple movie taught me a powerful lesson that I share with many. It is one of the reasons why it remains important to me to stay connected with the human element in all of my endeavors.

I'm not suggesting that adversity become a license for people to have a constant victim mentality and think that the world is out to get them, or to always have drama in their life. You've met some of these individuals, the people we know who are ALWAYS in a state of crisis. They let circumstances forever dictate their attitude, and complain that everyone else is to blame for their misery. Another Brandie-ism: **"The past doesn't give you a free pass to act like an ass!"**

To illustrate this point, I'm going to share one of my biggest personal emotional breakthroughs that happened seven years ago. By way of background, I'm the kind of person that when things go wrong in a relationship, I just want to blame myself, or at that time I was and did. I constantly asked, "What did I do wrong?" and "What could I have done differently?" Although some of those questions are healthy, I didn't always look at the reality that sometimes people make their own choices. People have their own issues going on in life that have nothing to do with me.

In fact, on many occasions, in the situation I experienced at that time, I realized I didn't matter that much to the other person, really. The person operated that way with everyone and everything in their life. I just happened to be the next person coming along. In truth, not everything was about ME. Go figure! Sometimes this thought helps me from taking on things that are not mine to be responsible for.

Your BY WHEN

Can you find out what's really going on with two people around you? Those around you, those you depend on. Be human first.

<u>Takeaways</u>

- People have their own issues to work through and their own challenges in life.
- There are people that may be going through tough times at home or tough times in their business.
- Maybe the people you deal with got some really bad news recently and they don't feel a need to share it with you.
- If you know what people are going through, you can choose to treat them with grace, forgiveness and respect.
- We often walk through life clueless about those around us.
- Adversity is not a license for people to have a constant victim mentality and always blame others.
- The past doesn't give you a free pass to act like an ass.
- Sometimes people make their own choices and have issues going on in life that have nothing to do with you.
- If something goes wrong in a relationship, the other person may operate that way with everyone and everything in their life.
- Not everything is about you.
- Don't take on things that are not yours to be responsible for.

The past doesn't give you a free pass to act like an ass!

Crossing the chasm

8

Crossing the Chasm

Let's review: At this point in our journey, you've analyzed your behaviors, your attitudes, and beliefs that formed them. You've considered how these opinions have changed over time. You may have even started to notice some of them changing because of these exercises.

You're making progress, but we have more to do.

All of this is preparing you to take action to achieve the change you sought by opening this book and completing the work thus far.

This leads me to what I call "Crossing the Chasm."

As we grow up, most of us are told, "If you (1) do all the right things, you will (2) have what you say you want and (3) you will be happy." A simple formula for success and happiness.

Perhaps your parents, teachers, or maybe even religious figures imprinted this message upon you. They may have stated the message many ways, but you understand the basic premise is the causal relationship between your behavior, your desires, and the results of satisfying those wants…in a word, happiness.

Here's a message that I received repeatedly "If you (1) do all your homework and get good grades, you will (2) have a degree

or credential, you will (3) be successful, and (4) you will be happy."
All forms of this message that you received (which may be slightly
different than what I was taught) have one thing in common.

It is an outright lie, a deception, to always equate achievement with happiness.

I'm sure the people who repeated these messages thought
they were helping, but experience teaches us there is absolutely
no direct relationship between these actions and the results
people promise. Think about it: If this formula proved true, only
those that achieve the most would have any semblance of happiness. Research has shown us that if you meet your basic needs,
additional achievement only produces marginal if any additional happiness. Often, high achievers harbor a secret: they're
supremely unhappy.

Even though I'm telling you the formula is a lie, and even
though I believe that it is, I still respond to it because I grew
up with it. Many of us did. We see the lie perpetuated through
our family upbringing, the media, our society, and in the workplace. We see the emphasis on *doing, doing, and more doing,*
yet we know people who can never do enough in their life to
be happy.

Friends have told me about an Instagram post that portrays a
coffee pot with the words, **"Your worth is not measured by your
productivity."**

Of course, we've all heard that people define success, and how
to achieve it, differently. For example, I will be successful if…

- I will be diligent
- I will be focused
- I will be content

If I possess any of these magic qualities, then I will *naturally* move through or I will omit things out of my life to achieve what I say I want.

I have struggled under this belief. Some of my belief system is still very geared around performance and doing. As you no doubt guessed, I am very task-oriented. I love getting things done. Knowing this about myself, I continue to take my own inventory and to redefine my decision to be happy and fulfilled.

Take a Break!

My husband said something very simple and profound for me. He said, "Brandie, there is always plenty to do. Take a break. Let's go outside, let's get out of here for a while and go do something – else! Else other than you working."

In his own way, my husband gave me the answer that had escaped me up until that moment. The embedded message that I had received—achievements lead to results, which lead to happiness—hampered my relationship in ways I didn't realize. It sometimes takes an external perspective, especially a loving one, to uncover this firmly held belief and to dislodge it from our firm grasp.

I'd love to report that from that time I have crossed my own chasm from my unhelpful beliefs, changed my behavior, all of which resulted in incredible fulfillment and joy. However, I'm not writing a novel or fairytale. The truth is from that point forward I've continued to change my belief and I have seen incremental improvements in my relationships and wellbeing. I know it is possible and I want this for you too!

Years ago one of my customers did the following as home-work and gave me one of the best examples I have seen of how someone took the concept I call "Crossing the Chasm" and implemented it into their life right away. He said:

> "I focused on times where I recognize that I needed to be in that **be**-ing instead of the **do**-ing. During the weekend following our discussion I focused on **be**-ing a father instead of **do**-ing activities with the kids. I was asked to participate in a program for parents of gifted children. Instead of agreeing to spearhead the program (the **do**-ing), I agreed to lead the brainstorming meeting and create a direction, allowing me to be accountable. I improved delegating recurring activities so I could be focused rather than **do**-ing the tasks. I drastically spent time on **be-i**ng organized. During our Wednesday office meeting I focused on **be**-ing direct, so that I wouldn't have to do more meetings clarifying my goals. During the time of significant change, I am trying to be a leader instead of **do**-ing a push on each employee. Since I'm still learning, I'm not certain whether that is what you are looking for. However, if it is, I am feeling comfortable with the concept, I just need more time for true habit-forming."

I deliberately include the unusual spellings of "**be**-ing" and "**do**-ing" to emphasize this person's shift in thinking.

To recap: Well-meaning people gave us the following formula for success.

- Do all the right things
- Have what you want
- Be happy.

Let's reverse-engineer this concept.

- Be who you'll choose to be—be happy, regardless of what you achieved.
- Do what makes you happy.
- Have what you want.

I want you to focus on who you're going to choose to be.

Are You Going to Be Happy?

The question is not predicated on having done enough homework (even mine!) to become happy, or attaining enough achievement to become happy. The real way to become happy is to choose to be a happy person, regardless of what you have or have not achieved. It may sound strange to suggest that happiness is a choice, but if you do a brief review, you'll begin to see the truth of this.

Look back on some of your other behaviors and the work we have done this far. Look at what you have written down on paper. You will be surprised at how much of your behavior is a choice you have made – to hold a certain belief or attitude far past its usefulness.

Your BY WHEN

Write down your belief structure on how you obtain happiness, fulfillment, or whatever your missing component seems to be. Then, look at how that has changed over time and where your chasm is to cross. Lastly, BY WHEN will you start to take the leap? Seriously. Write it down.

<u>Takeaways</u>

- Well-meaning people gave us the following formula for success: (1) Do all the right things to (2) have what you want and then you will (3) be happy. This is the "Do-Have-Be" formula. It is an outright lie, a deception, to always equate achievement with happiness.
- Many high achievers are supremely unhappy.
- Instead, choose the "Be-Do-Have" way. (1) Be who you'll choose to be—be happy, regardless of what you achieved, then (2) do or not do what makes you happy and you will (3) have what you want.
- Moving from "Do-Have-Be" to "Be-Do-Have" is called "Crossing the Chasm."
- The question is not predicated on having done enough homework (even mine!) to become happy, or attaining enough achievement to become happy.
- Choose to be a happy person, regardless of what you have or have not achieved.
- There is always plenty to do. Take a break.
- Focus on **be**-ing what you want instead of **do**-ing. If you want to improve your family life, focus on **be**-ing a father or mother rather than your to-do list.

Your worth is not measured
by your productivity.

MSU

9

MSU

How do you react in situations when you don't know what to do?

Many years ago, a friend and I had that very debate.

I said to my friend, "I believe there are two kinds of people. Miracle Whip™ people and Mayonnaise people." Then we began a hearty and friendly debate over this silly analogy:

"There are those who, when they don't know what to do, either (a) do something or (b) do nothing. There are **do**-ers and not **do**-ers. Miracle Whip™ or Mayonnaise. You can't be both."

I elevated The Miracle Whip™ people as those who do, or will at least venture an effort. Even if they are not sure how to respond, they will pick something to try. It may not be the best idea, but at least they choose action. They are the **do**-ers. They may accidentally pick the right response. On the other hand, it may have all gone horribly wrong and been completely inappropriate, but they acted.

The Mayonnaise people, those who do not do, get so discouraged because they don't know what to do that they do nothing at all.

I often remark that those that feel stuck need to become alumni of "MSU."

What does that stand for, you ask?

"Make Something Up."

Now for those of you who grew up in the South, like me, this is NOT what we call "making up a story" or lying.

Just come up with something—and move. Be committed. Try something. Do something. Open your mouth and say something without over-thinking—your brain will kick in, I promise. It really does happen! Inaction is worse than the consequences of failure.

The Real MSU: A Crash Course

A true story: I served on the faculty for a national training organization teaching a twenty-hour class held in Lansing, Michigan. And of course, if you travel often, you know that there are times you can't remember what city you're in or what day it is. This was one of those days.

I got off the plane and, after checking in to the hotel, went for a walk. I walked along the street observing green and white items everywhere: ball caps, toys, t-shirts, souvenirs…all bearing the logo "MSU".

And then it hit me. "Whoa! I'm at the home of Michigan State—MSU!"

I quickly seized the opportunity to solidify my "MSU" story with a bumper sticker, pin, and keychain that I use to remind me about MSU. I still have them all these years later.

I want to impart to you, through this story, the truth about fear and self-doubt. When we don't know what to do, many of us become afraid, and we often feel stuck and do not act. I have developed a four-step technique that helps me push through this fear.

Exercise

Consider the following scenario: A friend invites you to go hiking. You freeze and think of excuses not to accept.

Step One

Acknowledge that you feel self-doubt, fear, or whatever version of the emotion is present. Just recognize that these feelings occur within you in that moment you doubt yourself. In these instances, you may feel unsure what to say and unclear on how to act. Often your outward reality, what you respond to, depends on those around you and the makeup of those you interact with during such times.

In your internal analysis, you may think to yourself, "I don't even like hiking, but I don't want to look like a coward in front of this person." You fear looking foolish. However, you also acknowledge the rush of fear and emotions you feel when thinking about heights.

I've had these moments in my personal relationships. During these situations, I try to remember that men and women experience the same emotions—they just show it differently. I have confidence in the truth of that statement. Sometimes, ladies, we don't think men have emotions, but they do! And they feel the same things we feel. They just don't feel it all at the same time or in the same way, right?

Next, I want to give you some quick steps to overcoming the fear and initiating a response, or joining MSU if you will.

Step Two

I learned this technique years ago. I rate my fear level.

On a scale of one (not scared) to ten (horror-movie scared), how scared are you? Really? How much do you doubt yourself in this situation? Perhaps the current situation feels like a nine. If you see things again, more objectively, then maybe you rate the current situation as just a five. Self-awareness is key in overcoming these indecisive periods.

In our example, you rate your fear level as a nine or ten.

Step Three

Then I consider: "What's the worst possible thing that could happen? Like, really."

In our hiking example, you think to yourself, "What's the worst that can happen?"

You might think, "Well, I _could_ just fall off the cliff and die!"

A follow-up: "How afraid am I really? Is this a true nine, or merely a five masquerading as something larger?"

Ultimately, you must face what you're concerned about and issue your response.

Step Four

What can you do about your fears? What can you do to avoid the worst-case scenario?

My suggestion: Think about the worst outcome ahead of time and then focus on the steps you can take to avoid the worst thing from happening. Don't focus on it - just be aware of it so that if, during your hike, you happen to come across a cliff, you can say to yourself, "I've thought about this situation before and decided to remain calm."

Before you put on your hiking boots or shoes, you could ask those accompanying you if they hiked the trail previously. You could get information.

If you know that the trail involves cliffs, perhaps you ask to take a different trail.

In practice, meeting an unfamiliar scenario is always more difficult than one I've considered prior. A mental dress rehearsal before moments of stress and indecision often mitigates the level of fear enough to allow me to respond effectively.

So when your friend asks you to go hiking, use MSU and say, "Sure!"

Lastly, I pray the mayonnaise people (and the mayonnaise lawyers), as in the commercials, will not come for me after this.

<u>Your BY WHEN</u>

The next time you face indecision, pause to think about how scared you are on a scale of one to ten and try to be honest with yourself. Think about the worst-case scenario, and realize it is very unlikely. Prepare your mind and your body to be ready for the ensuing anxiety, remember that you are now a graduate from MSU. You now know how to make something up to move through it!

<u>Takeaways</u>

- How do you react in situations when you don't know what to do?
- I believe there are two kinds of people: those who, when they don't know what to do, either (a) do something or (b) do nothing.
- Those that feel stuck need to become alumni of MSU.
- MSU is not "making up a story" or lying.
- Just come up with something—and move. Be committed. Try something. Do something. Open your mouth and say something.
- Inaction is worse than the consequences of failure.
- Use a technique that helps you push through fear.
- Step One: Acknowledge that you feel self-doubt, fear, or whatever version of the emotion is present.
- Step Two: rate your fear level. On a scale of one to ten, how scared are you? Really? The current situation may feel like a nine on the scale but be a five.
- Step Three: Ask, "What's the worst possible thing that could happen? Like, really."
- Step Four: Use a mental dress rehearsal. Think about the worst outcome ahead of time and then focus on the steps you can take to avoid the worst thing from happening.

When you feel stuck, remember to MSU. Try to move off your normal pattern of thought and behavior and do something different.

YOU WILL **NEVER** BE **GOOD ENOUGH!**

10

"You Will Never Be Good Enough!"

The internal judgments we have about ourselves are much worse than any accusation anyone could make about us. These quiet opinions stop us from moving, from acting, from getting up and doing. Some of us fear others calling us a jerk or a pushover. Your internal dialogue may focus on the fear of friends/family/co-workers perceiving you as unreasonable or inflexible or unrealistic. If you start to monitor this process, you'll find your version and what you want to prevent the world from labeling you.

For years, I was so afraid of confrontation that I'd get physically sick. I would think, "IF I speak up, what will they think of me?" or "I'll never be as good as they are." Severe headaches and debilitative lower back pain began in high school. For those of you that normally have perfect health and notice physical things going on with your body, be open to noticing that that the backache or stomachache may result from internalizing emotion—in other words, from stress.

Think about it: We label someone as "a pain in the neck" or "a pain in the ass—or we call a situation "a headache." These expressions contain body wisdom! Our bodies can only handle so much emotion until it manifests in the form of pain.

Instead of focusing on my backache, I had to face the answer to the question, "What are you really afraid of?" The truth is that I feared that if I spoke up and shared my opinion, a contrary way of thinking to their status quo, or just sharing what I thought, that I would be ridiculed as someone who wasn't smart, business savvy or talented, or at the other extreme, as some hard-assed, inflexible, close-minded bitch. Strong language, but my internal monologue doesn't mince words. I had to face the reality that to get what I wanted in life, I had to be willing to make tough decisions and step out into my own identity, with the knowledge that not everyone would like me because of it.

Cure for a Backache and Headache

My back ached less when I started thinking about what I was afraid of. Then I imagined the worst-case scenario, and asked myself whether the worst-case scenario was genuinely possible (usually the answer was no). Then I considered my response ahead of time.

My lower back pain faded even more when I came to the realization that if people held that opinion of me, I would survive as long as I stayed true to myself and my values. I further realized that if I spoke up and they truly thought I was that horrible, that they didn't really know me at all. They didn't know the real me, the compassionate and caring me. I started thinking about whether their approval really mattered or if I could do anything about it.

I realized that I could be authentic and yet learn how to communicate in a different way that would reach others. I could learn the art and skill of language—and listening—and that's exactly what I did. I continue to work on those things presently. It is a lifelong endeavor.

The headaches and backache subsided and I noticed them less and less. I also read two great books, <u>Feelings Buried Alive Never Die</u> by Karol K. Truman and <u>Mind Over Back Pain</u> by John Sarno, M.D. Both of these helped me tremendously in finding my voice and learning to heal myself.

My technique of rating the risk and premeditating my response has helped me overcome some of my most debilitating fears. I'm proud to report that I no longer operate by allowing fear to corner me into inaction. Writing this book for all of you was one of those fears I needed to overcome.

I will tell you from personal experience that conquering the "never good enough" thoughts made a significant difference in my life. I am now willing to stand up, step up, step out and tell people, "This is who I am. This is what I'm not." The worst-case scenario for me is that I embarrass myself or offend people in the process. (And yes, I've still done both.) My preplanned response is to look at my words and deeds and take personal responsibility. I have done this publicly. These situations have made me stronger than I was previously. I'm able to confront or have an honest conversation with anyone, including being the one that people call on to facilitate their biggest challenges in dysfunctional workplaces.

<u>Your BY WHEN</u>

Write down five internal judgments you have about yourself. What are you afraid of being known as? Go through the process I mentioned earlier. Don't waste years the way I did being overly critical of yourself.

<u>Takeaways</u>

- We are harsher in judging ourselves than anyone else is.
- These quiet opinions stop us from moving, from acting, from getting up and doing.
- Buried emotions can cause physical ailments.
- Our bodies can only handle so much emotion until it manifests in the form of pain.
- Imagine the worst-case scenario and ask yourself whether the worst-case scenario is genuinely possible (usually the answer is no). Consider your response ahead of time.
- Realize that you will be okay as long as you stay true to yourself and your values regardless of what other people think.
- Be authentic, and yet communicate in a way that will reach others. Learn the art of connecting with authenticity.
- You can choose not to operate on your own paralyzing fears.

My preplanned response is to look at my words and deeds and take personal responsibility. These situations have made me stronger than I was previously.

Get in the car- how to overcome negative self-talk

11

How to Overcome Negative Self-Talk

This is a follow-up to the work you did in the last chapter. Take a look at those five negative judgments you wrote about yourself for that chapter's BY WHEN exercise. You might think, "Gosh, Brandie, only five? I usually have at least that many before breakfast."

I can relate. My internal monologue is often my most cruel and heartless critic—or as Queen of Your Own Life authors Kathy Kinney and Cindy Ratzlaff call it, the "Mongol Horde." If you notice the same pattern in your life, you may understand what I'm about to share with you. Many times, you may experience it as subconscious or background noise if you have dealt with it over a period of years Some individuals may not experience this form of self-talk, so if that's you, good on you.

Often, this negative self-image stems from environmental factors. If someone talked to you in a negative, demeaning way as a child or in a relationship, then you have a tendency sometimes to cling to those beliefs about yourself, and sometimes say things to yourself that frankly you would never allow anybody to say to you.

As a younger adult, I couldn't make a mistake without unleashing a barrage of negative self-talk. I would drop my napkin on the floor, spill my drink or trip over something and after I would make a klutzy mistake, I'd invariably say to myself:

- "Oh my gosh, you idiot!"
- "What is wrong with you?!"
- "You need to get it together."

Finally, I ended up talking to somebody about this, not in a padded room as you might have first imagined, but in my network. A wise advisor gave me an amazing visualization I call "Get in the Car" and it has dramatically changed my life and stopped that negative self-talk. In fact, I quit lifelong patterns in only <u>two weeks</u> and I'd like to share that with you today. In the previous chapter on negative self-talk, we identified the problem. Now, we take steps to overcome it

What my advisor shared with me was simple yet effective.

Exercise

Close your eyes and see yourself as if you have a twin sibling; like you're going to create a twin, an equal duplicate of yourself, except that person is always cynical and negative, saying bad things toward you such as, "You can't," or "You won't," or "You're not good enough."

In your mind, look at that person and say "Thank you for everything that you've done to help me in my life. But you know what? I'm going to try this on my own."

Then I want you to get in your car and drive away. Be aware that as you're looking in the rearview mirror of a car, your negative twin gets smaller and smaller and smaller.

Although this may seem simple, the next step is in being able to recognize the negative thoughts in your mind *when they are happening.* This will be difficult at first because they may have been running on auto-pilot for years without you realizing it. Once you can "hear" the specifics, you can do this exercise, as many times a day as you need to, until you notice the thoughts just going away and the frequency subsiding.

In my story, I chose to replace them with a sense of humor, laughing instead of feeling down on myself. Then I would rise up, go again, and press through.

Try it. Stay at it; this can be life changing for you as it was for me.

Your BY WHEN

Have your list of five negative self-judgments handy. When you catch yourself saying any of those to yourself, or any other internal criticism, do the Exercise. To recap:

1. Stop.
2. Look at that person.
3. Thank them for their way of trying to help you.
4. Tell them that you figured everything out.
5. Get in the car, drive away and watch that person get smaller and smaller and smaller

Repeat as often as needed to overcome some of that negative self-talk. It worked for me; it has worked for so many people that I have coached and helped over the years and I hope it helps you as well.

<u>Takeaways</u>

- Take a look at your five negative self-judgments.
- Your internal monologue is often your most cruel and heartless critic.
- Negative self-talk often stems from people talking to you in a negative, demeaning way.
- You sometimes say things to yourself that frankly you would never allow anybody to say to you.
- A visualization I use, "Get in the Car," is a simple but effective way to quit negative self-talk.
- When you hear negative self-talk, imagine your negative twin saying those hurtful things to you.
- Stop. Look at your negative twin.
- Thank them for helping you and tell them you figured everything out.
- Get in the car, drive away and leave the negative twin/ self-talk in the rearview mirror. Repeat as often as needed.

*Check out
https://powerhouselearning.com/
videos-and-podcasts to see me
describe this process in person*

A WARNING ABOUT THE CONSEQUENCES OF POSITIVE CHANGE

12

A Warning About the Consequences of Positive Change

Congratulations! You've done some hard work up to this point.

You've identified the true obstacles to change, using the Price I PAY vs. what I GET.

You've spent time considering the position of others in your life.

With your vision solidified and all the clarity you can muster, you stand ready to profess your new resolution – to herald your triumph from atop the office water cooler.

Before you triumphantly ascend the water dispenser, a word of caution:

Remember that just because you have had a defining moment, don't assume the same about others around you. I see this misguided belief every day as I work with organizations that experience major breakthroughs in their business and create positive change.

Just because a department leader is ready to change or one person in a family is ready to change, this doesn't mean that everybody else feels as excited about change, does the research or invests the time getting ready to change or to make the next step.

Often, I explain this scenario using the fictional if not farcical sitcom-like trip to Joe's Bar. Imagine that every day after work, we meet up at Joe's Bar and we commiserate about how much you hate your job, how much I hate my job, and so on. One day I stride up to my normal perch and say, "Well I just want to let you know that my husband and my family are not happy with me because - insert air quotes – apparently I have a drinking problem! I can't meet with you at the bar anymore and in fact tomorrow I won't be here at all. I'm going to be over at the park. Want to meet me at the park instead?"

Suddenly, you feel as if I'm imposing my own change and decisions on you and they are affecting your life. After all, you wanted to go to the bar after work and kvetch about the workplace while killing brain cells. You didn't sign up for an uplifting walk in the park. My choice to sober up forces you to do the same by default, because I won't be meeting at Joe's to whine about life and work anymore, if you choose to follow me. My decision forces a life change in you, if you wish to participate.

Fast-forward to the next day and I don't go to Joe's Bar. Instead, I decide to go to the park.

In response, you choose to do one of the following:

a) Reluctantly show up at the park with all your disappointment in tow.

b) Show up to Joe's Bar (maybe even with a new office comrade).

c) Go straight home.

You can probably guess what happens to our friendship next. We no longer meet up. You don't want to talk about drinking for fear of judgment and I don't want to watch you drink as I try to wean myself from Grandpa's old cough medicine.

I've just presented a precautionary tale about change. Don't let this warning deter you, but do take note that just because you're very motivated and ready to make steps into the right direction doesn't mean everyone else will be on board.

Think about how you communicate your change initiates to people, and give them time to process, just as you have made necessary steps over time to read, learn, contemplate and think through the action steps.

Your **BY WHEN**

Consider the change your team (or family, or friends) will have to make in response to the change you are making. Your actions compel them to be different. Write down examples of their responses. Try to build empathy for their position.

Takeaways

- You've done the hard work up to this point and are ready to profess your new resolution.
- Remember that just because you have had a defining moment, don't assume the same about others around you.
- Just because a department leader is ready to change or one person in a family is ready to change, this doesn't mean that everybody else feels as excited about change.
- Positive change has consequences for your relationships. Don't let this deter you.
- Consider the change your team will have to make in response to the change you are making.
- Have empathy for people's reactions.

UNKNOWN UNKNOWNS

13

The Unknown Unknowns

I remember watching television sometime in 2002 and seeing Secretary of Defense Donald Rumsfeld awkwardly talk about this thing called "don't know that you don't know" when referencing a situation between U.S. and Iraqi relations.

His clumsily spoken declaration went something like this, "There are known knowns. These are things we know that we know. There are known unknowns. That is to say, there are things that we know we don't know. But there are also unknown unknowns. There are things we don't know we don't know." The press went wild asking, "What the heck was he talking about?!"

Years before I had learned a little bit about this saying, something along these lines:

- There are things in life that we KNOW THAT WE KNOW – the smallest bit of information.
- There are things that we KNOW THAT WE DON'T KNOW – yet a bit larger.
- Lastly, things that we DON'T KNOW THAT WE DON'T KNOW – the largest amount of information available both about ourselves and about others and the world around us.

It seems rather silly but then I started thinking about it. Take, for example, the fact that *I know that I know* how to drive a car. I often say that if you have ridden with me you would dispute that fact! Nonetheless, *I know that I don't know* how to drive a tractor. I think it looks fascinating, but I have never had the desire to learn. Then there are things in life that I just do*n't know that I don't know:* things that I do, nuances I have, opportunities that I miss in life, etc. For example, I could habitually text while driving (dangerous!) and not realize I'm doing it.

I often ask people, "Do you think you are accountable for what you don't know that you don't know?" I always get a variety of answers. Some say, "No, we can't be because we're not aware of what we don't know." Other people, however, recognize that we are accountable for what Donald Rumsfeld called our "unknown unknowns" because of the effect our actions (or lack of) have on others.

Let me give you an example. Years ago, I was asked to facilitate strategic conversations with an international shoe company. Julie, the director of operations, grew up through the ranks and I saw her as a very sharp young lady, 5' 11", beautiful, insightful and completely distracted. She would often begin meetings with her long waist-length blond hair high up in a ponytail, and once discussion became more challenging she would pull her hair tie all the way through that long blonde hair and begin twiddling with her hair, twisting it in knots, then gathering it up again and putting it away in a completely new ponytail.

After the second hour, I finally could not stand it any longer! I asked her, "Julie, I am sure that you work with many businesspeople both here in the United States and overseas, is that correct?"

She answered, "Yes, of course."

To which I replied, "So do you think when you do this thing with your hair that you earn *more respect* or *less respect* from the people in these business meetings?"

This helped Julie think about and be mindful of her unconscious, nervous habit.

Let's review the question, "Do you think you are accountable for what you don't know that you don't know?" In my case, the answer is a *yes*.

That leads me to the next point—how do we find out what we *don't know that we don't know*?

Well, I believe there are only two ways.

1. **Self-mastery**, or the willingness to read, listen and engage with other people and learn ways that you can grow and develop as a person.

2. **Honest feedback**. The gift of feedback allows us to receive information even though we don't necessarily like the message. That information tells us things that maybe we are not aware of, the things that others observe about us, and sometimes, the things that hold us back from becoming all we are meant to become.

Your BY WHEN

How can you find out more about what you don't know that you don't know? Focus on discovering the habits, language, and style of communication that you may be using that you are not aware affects your relationships.

<u>Takeaways</u>

- There are things in life that we KNOW THAT WE KNOW – the smallest bit of information, such as knowing how to drive a car.
- There are things that we KNOW THAT WE DON'T KNOW – yet a bit larger, such as not knowing how to drive a tractor.
- Also, there are things that we DON'T KNOW THAT WE DON'T KNOW – the largest amount of information available both about ourselves and about others and the world around us, such as unconsciously texting while driving.
- We are accountable for what we don't know that we don't know.
- We can observe others to find out what they don't know they don't know about themselves.
- We can learn about our unknown unknowns through self-mastery, or the willingness to read, listen and engage with other people and learn ways that you can grow and develop as a person.
- We can also learn through honest feedback about things that maybe we are not aware of, the things that others observe about us, and sometimes, the things that hold us back from becoming all we are meant to become.
- Focus on discovering the habits, language, and style of communication that you may be using that you are not aware affects your relationships.

There are many rewards, and challenges, that come from discovering more of what you Don't Know That You Don't Know – but they are worth it if you are open to the feedback!

Hamster Wheel

14

The Hamster Wheel

The Hamster Wheel.

I'm referring to that incessant thought process racing through the mind, consuming brain cycles like a rapacious creditor. You may have a different phrase.

The Hamster Wheel goes around and around and around and doesn't stop. The wheel represents something that is bothering me, thoughts I can't stop, playing out scenarios past or future. Those that suffer under the weight of the hamster wheel know what I'm talking about: the thoughts that won't go away, the things that keep you up at night. Clinicians probably have a pill for this, but let me explain why it is useful.

The *Wheel de Hamster*, if you will, is a powerful life principle about not letting your thoughts run wild and overwhelm you. You have the power within you to stop this.

To counteract this process, I focus my attention on establishing the reality of what I can and can't control. I put aside things outside of my control as much as possible, and spend my energy working on the parts I can affect. I harness my ideas and allocate time to attending to them.

If you, like me, have a lot of creative thoughts, keep a notebook next to your bed and the next time you wake up in the middle of the night, write down enough bullet points so you can recall the flow of things the next morning. If that does not work, write down the things that you can control and those you can't, or what you can do and what you can't. Set those things aside that are outside your control. Instead, focus on the power within you to react or act when things get tough.

You probably know people who brag about being busy and you catch yourself wearing it as a badge of honor. Telling others we are busy makes us feel important, yet I caution you against it. Obsessing by having your *Head Up Your Phone* at all times does the same thing. After all, aren't we all busy? Declaring the obvious can actually distance relationships with your peers and clients. Stop telling people you are "swamped," "overwhelmed," "have so much on your plate" and "have a lot going on. Great leaders do not stoop to this place; they find ways to be better at managing their energy and creating space to be balanced. Please have the courage to stop the Hamster Wheel and just relax your mind— you probably need a good sleep. After completing the homework thus far, you deserve one!

Your BY WHEN (For Hamsters)

What problems or thoughts cause you to focus on activities that lead nowhere? What thoughts spin endlessly through your mind? Are you spending mental resources on situations you cannot change? List the aspects that are under your control and double down on addressing those.

Takeaways

- The Hamster Wheel represents endlessly repeating thoughts about situations that bother you, thoughts you can't stop.
- The Hamster Wheel represents the things that keep you up at night.
- The Hamster Wheel is a useful, powerful life principle about not letting your thoughts run wild and overwhelm you.
- Focus your attention on establishing the reality of what you can and can't control.
- Set aside things outside of my control as much as possible, and spend your energy working on the parts you can affect.
- If you have a lot of creative thoughts, keep a notebook next to your bed and the next time you wake up in the middle of the night, write down enough bullet points so you can recall the flow of things the next morning.
- Or write down the things that you can control and those you can't, or what you can do and what you can't.
- Don't get addicted to needing to feel busy even in your own mind and thoughts. Stop telling people you are "overwhelmed." Stop the Hamster Wheel, get your head out of your phone, and get some rest!

SECTION II

5 Action Steps

Disappointment Algorithm

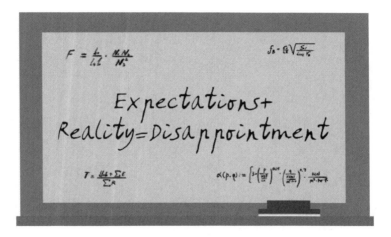

1

Disappointment Algorithm

For those of you seeking concrete quantifiable results from this book, I'm going to share with you one of the most important equations I've stumbled upon. I referred to this algorithm twice before in the chapter on Conversations For Action (C4A)—especially when referring to parents expecting kids to clean up their rooms.

I've summed up the entirety of human experience in the form of a simple arithmetic equation:

$$\text{Expectations} + \text{Reality} = \text{Disappointment}.$$

OK, maybe I oversold this, but you may still find it helpful. Here's how it works. We start with expectations, often fantasized expectations, of how we want the world to look. Add to these expectations a clear dose of reality, or "What is SO." Often, we find ourselves disappointed, likely because we haven't articulated or communicated our expectations.

A quote from the movie *Enchanted* says, "I know how it is when someone disappoints you. It's tempting to see things the way you wish they were instead of how they are."

That's why we face disappointment when we hear things such as:

- "Hey, let's have lunch sometime."
- "We'll talk then."
- "Ten o'clock Monday?" "Great."
- "We need to talk."
- "You need to get your numbers up."
- "We need to get the house cleaned."

That kind of communication does little except set up expectation for disappointment because we are lacking our BY WHEN.

True story: One of the worst groundings I ever got happened when my mother said, "We need to get the house cleaned."

Hearing this most of my life and knowing what it meant, I quipped, "Do you mean 'we' or just 'me'—AS USUAL?!?"

If you chuckled at that, I'm grateful for the weeks spent staring at the walls of my bedroom while my friends went out and had fun. If you learned something, I have to thank my mom for that story. In my own snarky teenage way, I introduced BY WHEN.

BY WHEN changes everything. It fixes vague, ambiguous conversation into specificity. I've worked with thousands of people that have seen transformation in their communication. I can assure you that this simple phrase will lead you to a lot less disappointment if you learn to use this technique.

Let me give you a business example: You hire a new person in your department. You think the new hire has all the credentials they stated or represented on their resume and during the interview process. The new hire shows bright promise for the first couple weeks, the first couple of months. He/she certainly seems smart enough, ambitious enough…then **nothing**. They stop being productive. BOOM. DISAPPOINTMENT.

That new employee that you had so much hope for is now underperforming, seemingly overnight—but in reality, nothing changed. Or perhaps what changed is that the employee, seeing that you have created or accepted a culture of mediocrity, stopped trying so hard. After all, most everyone else isn't pushing hard, so why should the new employee meet your expectations?

Please remember this important lesson: our thoughts (and disappointment) are based on whose expectations? That's right, **our** expectations. **Our** expectations are based on our belief system, our filters about our way of relating to life. They are **ours**.

The other party has come into the situation with whose expectations? That's right, **not** ours—**_theirs_**, with their own filters, their own way of relating to life, **not** yours.

In this scenario, unless you sit down and create alignment through questions, listening, and agreement, you will have lasting disappointment and busted ambition. Said another way, if you want to use the soft-skill term, you have low morale. If you want to use a no-nonsense term, you're losing your ass on profitability. Disappointment, 'tis yours.

Don't fall victim to that lasting and universal equation I just provided. Don't let your expectations plus reality equal disappointment. Use this formula to analyze your vision and change your result to satisfaction.

Your BY WHEN

Add up the expectations that when in the light of reality turned into absolute chaos. Analyze your past experiences and grow from them.

Takeaways

- We start with expectations, often fantasized expectations, of how we want the world to look. Add to these expectations a clear dose of reality, or what I call "What is SO."
- Often, we find ourselves disappointed, likely because we haven't articulated or communicated our expectations.
- We often don't communicate our expectations using our BY WHEN.
- BY WHEN changes everything.
- Our thoughts (and disappointment) are based on **our** expectations, which are based on our belief system, our filters about our way of relating to life. They are **ours**.
- The other party has come into the situation with their expectations, with their own filters, their own way of relating to life.
- Unless you sit down and create alignment through questions, listening, and agreement, you will have low morale and lose your ass on profitability.
- Don't let your expectations plus reality equal disappointment. Use this formula to analyze your vision and change your result to satisfaction.

Take a look at areas you feel disappointed in people or circumstances in life. What can you do to realign your expectations or communicate differently in order to achieve a different result?

My Least Favorite Word

2

My Least Favorite Word

My least favorite word in the English language (or any other language I speak) is COMMUNICATION.

It never fails: every survey I've seen in every size organization always includes a section on "communication."

Invariably, communication ranks in the top five most frustrating things for the management teams of organizations we consult with nationwide. We see "lack of communication" indicated on survey results within every department. Whether the employees work in accounting, operations, sales or marketing, no matter the department, "lack of communication" always tops the list of grievances.

A caveat: My aversion to this word does not stem from my lack of appreciation for its importance as a topic but rather how leaders use it to avoid soliciting or listening to honest feedback and criticism.

Case Study: Steve the Communicator

My client Steve, a 62-year-old business owner, monopolized our first introduction by repeating, "You know, I'm not a good communicator." If we made a movie, Woody Allen would definitely play Steve.

Like any Woody Allen character, Steve, in my opinion, seemed very capable on the surface. He has run a very successful small business for over forty years. He is well known and well respected in his community and by his many hundreds of customers. However, Steve has a problem with authority—his own.

Initially, I found it difficult to believe Steve labeling himself "not a good communicator" because he had such an incredible reputation. Something didn't add up, so I asked him, "Explain to me what you mean by 'communication' because there are only two or three ways to communicate."

He then shared that it was more about him keeping other people informed and in the loop. It was also about how he connected with and motivated family that worked in the business.

The leadership surveys of Steve, Inc., revealed all parties saying they struggle most with "communication" and that it was tearing the business apart. I thought, "What the heck is really going on over there?"

When I dug deeper, I began to understand that "communication" was just another bad "c" word for broken trust, disheveled ambition, broken promises, missed expectations and lack of a solid plan for the future.

The sad part: The management's lack of willingness to get out of their own way dramatically affected the staff's confidence in ANY of them as leaders.

Oftentimes, "lack of communication" represents selfish behavior where individuals only think about themselves and don't include others in the daily loop, even if those happenings affect the selfsame parties that are being excluded! Worse, we find that the perception that it will take longer, or that we don't have time to communicate, will come back and bite us in the butt. The consequences of not learning how to properly bring people along in the process from the beginning include an extreme amount of make-up time, that exact thing which we avoided from the start by not communicating in the first place!

Know this: communication problems in organizations are surprisingly easy to address. The techniques contained in the earlier chapter on Conversations For Action (C4A) will correct communication conundrums.

This process does not run smoothly at the start because you are retraining decades of accepted "normal." See the chapter on "Consequences of Positive Change" for secrets on making this work without tearing your hair out. Yes, you will have some disappointment as you move into clarity and retraining the way people's minds connect words with actions. However, you will be amazed at the results – and I'm talking quick results that are *sustainable* with less effort than you thought possible.

Sales & Marketing: A Problem Area

I love retraining Sales and Marketing teams. These individuals are responsible for generating revenue and getting the word out about how exceptional your organization is. In essence, they communicate for a living. In an interesting twist of irony, internal staff often accuse them of ineffective communications.

The most common communication problem in Sales and Marketing: Too often the departments don't generate alignment with their prospects or customers and their own firm's internal capabilities. In other words, if the customers expect better widgets at lower prices and the firm can't deliver what a marketing rep promises, disappointment results.

In the pursuit of commissions and goals imposed by management, Sales and Marketing routinely chase deals far beyond the point at which any sane individual would tap out. This results in a disjointed series of broken promises that other departments must scramble to correct. In their departments, salespeople and marketing professionals often struggle with:

- Poor Planning
- Poor Attitude
- Lack of Continuous Training and Education
- Poor Time Management
- Lack of Written Goals
- Lack of Discipline
- Poor Self-Analysis

To compound the problem, many organizations feel the need to purchase and deploy technology in a feeble attempt to address what is a decidedly non-technological problem. The bosses deploy Customer Relationship Management software and magically expect all departments to master this new technology in hopes that the communication woes of the manual age will soon be a distant memory. In practice, few organizations that install these systems and generate reports use the tool for their benefit. Companies have spent millions of dollars on the deception that managers forcing the need for reports will influence and change behavior.

Our teams need only learn a very simple new language to affect change, the language you are learning here. No software required. Creating conversations that drive action is the solution. Silicon Valley has yet to create the computer system that will shape employees' behavior from a deep understanding of their preconceived and engrained attitudes and assumptions. The problem does not lend itself to a technological solution.

To illustrate the often messy, complicated and rewarding dynamics of communication, let me share this fable (slightly adapted here).

Frogs

A group of frogs traveled through the woods one day, and two of them fell into a deep pit. All the other frogs gathered around the pit. When the group saw how deep the pit was, the frogs all told their two friends, "You're as good as dead."

The two frogs ignored the comments and tried to jump up out of the pit with all of their might. The other frogs kept telling them to stop, that they were as good as dead.

Finally, one of the frogs took heed to what the other frogs were saying and gave up. He fell down and died. The other frog continued to jump as hard as he could. Once again, the crowd of frogs yelled at him, "Stop the pain, make it easier on yourself and just die."

He jumped even harder and finally made it out.

When he got out, the other frogs said, "Didn't you hear us?"

(I LOVE THIS PART) The frog explained to them that he was hard of hearing and *thought they were cheering him on the whole time.*

This story teaches <u>two</u> lessons:

There is *power of life and death* in the tongue.

1. An <u>encouraging</u> word to someone who is down can lift them up and help them make it through the day.

2. A <u>destructive</u> word to someone who is down can be what it takes to kill them.

"Be careful of what you say. Speak life to those who cross your path.
It's sometimes hard to understand that an encouraging
word can go such a long way."
—Author Unknown

I would add a third moral to that story: Sometimes what counts is what people hear, not what you say. So be clear! Have those Conversations for Action.

Also, a fourth moral: Turning your (figurative) hearing aid off to negative talk can be helpful!

Your BY WHEN

What communication logjams can you articulate within your organization? Identify the key players and the steps needed to use what you've learned thus far to outline some action steps.

Takeaways

- Leaders use the word "communication" to avoid soliciting or listening to honest feedback and criticism.
- "Communication" is just another bad "c" word for broken trust, disheveled ambition, broken promises, missed expectations and lack of a solid plan for the future.
- Oftentimes, "lack of communication" represents selfish behavior where individuals only think about themselves and don't keep others in the daily loop about events and information that affect everyone.
- The techniques contained in the earlier chapter on

Conversations For Action (C4A) will correct communication conundrums.

- Expect the process to not run smoothly at first because in the beginning, you retrain decades of accepted "normal," but you can retrain belief systems.

- Many companies deploy Customer Relationship Management software and magically expect all departments to master this new technology as a quick fix for communication problems. This rarely works.

- Sometimes what counts is what people hear, not what you say. So be clear! Have those Conversations for Action.

The Seed You Plant Is The Crop You Get

3

The Seed You Plant is the Crop You Get

This is a life principle and a spiritual principle.

As noted, I reside in rural Idaho and see all kinds of crops grow during different seasons. Each year, I see corn, beans, alfalfa (hay), wheat, barley, sugar beets (often used to sweeten the food we eat), and, of course, potatoes.

This farm story has a point. During my day job, wherever I travel, I listen to many people and organizations talk about what is broken or what's not working within their company. I love being known as a person who affects positive change. However, often-times that change comes when good people face a tough reality.

You know how it all starts, with a lot of talk and energy and complaining about what's not working; who is not doing their part. Customers routinely proclaim that they have had enough of the nonsense, the mediocrity, the lack of accountability, etc. but they don't tell you directly; they just leave (and they lie and tell you it's about getting a better price).

Years ago, to illustrate this life principle I started talking about corn and green beans. I started saying, "The seed you plant is the crop you get! Sometimes people plant corn and expect green beans. When the cornstalk starts coming out of the ground, they say, 'What the heck is that?! That's not what I planted!'"

In the business environment, the same complaint sounds like this: "I'm a good person, a good leader, and I do what I'm supposed to, we just can't seem to get anyone else around here to do what they're supposed to." Each captain will tell you they execute, yet that is not what everyone sees showing up or manifesting or being produced in the results. And often, everyone else gets the blame.

I love the last scene in the movie *Secondhand Lions* with Robert Duvall and Michael Caine. Both of them (neither were farmers, of course) had been duped into thinking that they had planted a varied garden full of vegetables. They labeled each perfectly manicured row with a different vegetable, and even placed a little picture on a small wooden stake at the beginning of each row. They faithfully tilled and watered and weeded the garden, and waited with great anticipation for harvest, only to see corn come up in every single row, over and over again.

Michael Caine as Garth says, "That's SOME lion you bought," and Robert Duvall as Hub says, "Huh. SOME garden seeds YOU bought!"

If you haven't seen the movie, it's worth seeing, for many other reasons than this.

This story is a metaphor for life. Many leadership teams wait too long to find out that they planted the wrong seeds.

Pulling all that corn up can be painful, but many people avoid making that mistake over and over again if they learn the lesson to pay attention to the results (or lack thereof) a lot sooner. Just remember to start by looking in the mirror to identify what you can do differently as a leader to get a different result, or crop, in your organization or department. If you need help seeing or hearing what your crop is, refer back to your most recent surveys, or even better, what you're complaining the most about!

Your (Farm Fresh) BY WHEN

Get to planting! Oh, and pay attention to the seeds. What have you planted and what is growing in your "field"? No, seriously. Write it down.

Takeaways

- Change often comes when people face a tough reality.
- The seed you plant is the crop you get. You can't plant corn and expect green beans.
- People say they are planting one crop, yet they get a different result and blame others for it. Take a look in the mirror first to identify what you can do differently.
- Watch the movie *Secondhand Lions*.
- Many leadership teams wait too long to find out that they planted the wrong seeds.
- Pulling all that corn up can be painful, but many people avoid making that mistake over and over again if they learn the lesson to pay attention to the results (or lack thereof) a lot sooner.
- If you need help seeing or hearing what your crop is, refer back to your most recent frustrations and complaints.

Accountability Is A Cinch, Really

4

Personal Responsibility vs. Accountability, and the Need For Appreciation

Sometimes in relationships, when we're having a conflict, the fault may be contributory, not necessarily proportionate. In other words, when you're in a relationship with another human being, you're obviously connected to them in one way or another. When you two have a conflict, you shouldn't just make it all about that other person.

If I allow for the possibility that I may have caused a reaction that I wasn't aware of, I know there's a lot of wisdom to gain in being able to objectively pick apart these kinds of situations, own what's mine, and leave the rest. We call that taking personal responsibility.

If you have a part in communication logjams (that would be all of us, by the way), own up.

However, managers often mix up responsibility with accountability.

Think about it: I cannot make a promise to myself—we call that a resolution. Similarly, I cannot be accountable to myself. I can only be personally responsible for my actions. I can, however, support another person by helping them be accountable in their own resolutions or their objectives.

Case Study: Jane's Accountability

Jane was part of a multigenerational business in the Midwest started by her father who has since passed. Although the business had survived wars, economic downturns, changing consumer behaviors and all manner of culture changes over the years, the family members running the operation were slowly tearing the business apart.

Thankfully, Jane possessed enough self-awareness to reach out for help to bring peace back to the family enterprise.

This is a cautionary tale about simple language we commonly use, such as words like accountability or responsibility, getting in the way of what we really want.

The first comments the members made when we opened the dialogue began with the phrases: "in my defense" or "in her defense."

The fact that every member chose to start our deliberation this way highlighted the need to address this subtle but troublesome habit. The sad truth was that they often did not support one another and so they resorted to language like "in my own defense."

I asked each member during the strategic planning session why they even needed to defend themselves in the first place! Of course, I got an earful of all the dysfunction that was going on behind the scenes. Those without motive lack the need to headline their comments with such declarations. After getting past the attitudes that shaped the beliefs and the desire for self-exoneration, we began to make real progress finding the common ground and the purpose that everyone could agree on.

The people in Jane's scenario took no personal responsibility and also did not make themselves accountable to Jane or each other. There also was no appreciation—although this changed greatly by the time we finished working together.

Appreciation

Managers and leaders universally adore accountability. I often remind leaders of my phrase "When you have Agreement, you have (better) Accountability." But remember, you don't have to use it like a hammer. I also know that staff and sales teams want to be shown appreciation for how they contribute.

Please stop assuming your team is not human. Also stop assuming they are solely motivated by money. In fact, if the money statement were true we would not have plateaued-out executives all over the country, nor would we have so many problems internally within organizations. When you talk about accountability, don't forget the other "a" word: Appreciation.

Your staff wants to be shown appreciation in the way they understand and receive it, not in your way, remember? Sales and Marketing teams would really like to hear positive feedback receive recognition from their peers, so give them an audience to share their experiences. Highlight them publicly in your regular meetings and give them a forum to bask in the adulation from the rest of the team. Remember so many employees thrive on public acknowledgement, not just their private commission statements and paychecks.

Effective leaders use their regular meetings to highlight the individual members of the team. A manager who dominates and absorbs the attention throughout the entire gathering risks alienating the very people they are trying to motivate. Use your meetings to focus on the individual members and plan ahead to create the right setting for their success. Also, give them a little love. Let me explain what I mean.

Love Languages

Years ago, Gary Chapman wrote a book called <u>The 5 Love Languages</u>, a breakthrough piece on how each of us experience love and appreciation through our own filters and in our own way. It's only five things and so easy to remember. Although Chapman wrote it with personal relationships in mind, I believe it applies just as appropriately in business relationships.

Consider reading <u>The 5 Love Languages</u>, especially if you are in a personal or business relationship with any other human being. If you are a manager, motivating people and helping them become accountable does not really have to be difficult. All you have to do is ask and listen, and I can guarantee that every member of your team fits into one of the five categories that Chapman mentions in his work. Find ways of how this connects in a professional environment.

Your BY WHEN

Write down what you are *responsible* for and the people you are *accountable* to. Also, think of ways you can show appreciation to the people in your life.

Takeaways
- Managers often mix up responsibility with accountability.
- You cannot be accountable to yourself. You can only be personally responsible for your actions.

- You can support another person by helping them be accountable in their own resolutions or their objectives.
- Managers and Leaders universally adore accountability but don't use it like a hammer.
- When you have agreement, you have (better) accountability.
- Please stop assuming your team is not human. Also stop assuming they are solely motivated by money.
- Your staff wants to be shown appreciation in the way they understand and receive it.
- If you are a manager, motivating people and helping them become accountable does not really have to be difficult. All you have to do is ask and listen.

A Strange Way
to Build Confidence

A Strange Way To Build Confidence

Through taking a stand, I found a strange way to build confidence for myself and for others. After coaching hundreds of sales and account service teams, their principals and leaders, I realized something very powerful, and it came in the most bizarre way.

A few years ago, I did a routine update of one of our websites and needed to sift through the information. As I read our testimonials I started seeing a pattern. The word "confidence" kept popping up. Our team helped bring people confidence to make the changes that they needed to make—and of course, the clients were getting incredible results. They said they felt confident because of our time with them and that confidence translated into action, which produced results.

Suddenly, I realized **confidence and accountability are connected!**

Confidence motivates accountability—and results.

I said, "Sheesh, I don't really see myself as a motivational speaker type." And yet, the feedback was undeniable.

Then it hit me...the method we use to create the accountability conversation made all the difference.

What this means is that setting a deadline and bringing it to their attention when they did not deliver was showing them I was interested in the exchange and that the agreement was genuinely important to fulfill.

The business lesson for me? You can wield accountability as a hammer and never achieve sustained initiative, avoid the conflict and see delayed results, or use language as incentive and watch your team grow. Take the incentive route. Stay with your team and care enough to see them through to the achievement of their goals. Implement the required components to make lasting change possible.

Your (confidence building) BY WHEN

Review the last time you set a deadline with your team, coworker, or family member. Did you use the hammer or the incentive? What could you have done differently? Spend the time now to understand the process and put the hammer away.

Takeaways

- Accountability builds confidence.
- You can wield accountability as a hammer or avoid the conversation altogether and never achieve sustained initiative.
- Stay with your team and care enough to see them through to the achievement of their goals. Implement the required components to make lasting change possible.

SECTION III

8 Ways to Share With Others

Difficult Conversations

1

Difficult Conversations

Conflict polarizes people into two camps: those who move toward the disagreement and those who avoid or move away from it.

In polite society, we tend to emphasize avoiding difficult conversations. You can remember a discussion with a colleague or a loved one that didn't go well. Your instinct was likely to withdraw from conflict and postpone or evade the issue entirely. To maximize productivity and personal growth, we have to be able to address these situations as they arise and make them fruitful.

If we stop to look at the elements that make these discussions so arduous, we uncover internal conflict as well as external conflict that often skate under the radar. Adding to the confusion, each person has an emotional response and favored method to address tense discourse that may add fuel to the awkwardness.

Further, your initial approach to handling conflict differs based on certain personality characteristics. Some people identify as more introverted, others more extroverted. Also, those that operate on emotions as opposed to rational deliberation will naturally butt heads about how best to proceed.

It's important to prepare you to make the most of these situations that will invariably arise in your daily interactions. I'm going to walk you through some very specific ways to handle difficult conversation in a healthy way and to achieve the desired result for yourself and for the other party.

The Four Basic Secret Needs

The first step in addressing difficult conversations is to learn how to correctly interpret others' motivations. Trouble starts at this phase. If you look carefully, listen, and pay attention, you can begin to recognize the clues given by speech patterns, choice of words or phrases, body language, and personality type.

In terms of motivation, humans have very similar reasons for doing most things. Categorically, we are not much different in our needs, at least as far as conversations are concerned. All of us have four basic hidden needs:

1. to feel welcome
2. to be understood
3. to feel important
4. to feel comfortable and at ease.

Keeping these motivations in mind, we move in the direction of resolution by asking, "How can we fulfill these needs in each party?" When conflicts arise, invariably, one or both parties have stepped on or ignored one of these four areas of fundamental human motivation.

If one party responds with aggression or contempt, the other naturally withdraws. It is crucial that both parties address this fundamental mismatch. If the other party is being the aggressor, I have two choices: continue to engage or withdraw. The situation becomes awkward either way. However, by recognizing that the other party may feel just as uncomfortable as you, we begin to look at the next problem with having these conversations.

To be understood, to have your point of view or opinion acknowledged and appreciated, is crucial to any interaction. If both people blindly insist on their position taking priority, the discussion usually devolves into argument. By addressing this with the other party, we move into a better position to have our point heard.

Each party wants to feel that his or her position and time is important. We can be dismissive if we have differences of opinion. However, if I disagree with your position, the least effective tactic is to trivialize your view. Going into a difficult discussion, you may find it critical not to disregard the opposing view or let a flippant comment derail an otherwise useful interaction.

No one likes conflict. Tension is not a comfortable state of mind, and people prefer comfort to uneasiness. When we have conflicts, we're naturally motivated to regain homeostasis in our relationships—and to break the silence.

If you've ever had a disagreement with a spouse, you know how deafening and uncomfortable silence can be when two parties have conflict. If you clam up, remember that your spouse also has a desire to regain comfort, and cold silence is the opposite of being comfortable. Resolution is possible if we don't continue to feed into the tension by employing methods such as silent scorn. And if you pay attention to the four secret needs I listed earlier, and keep in mind each party's motivation.

What's Your Motivation? What's Your Style?

Once we get clear about the motivation behind the conflict, we can then analyze the differences in personalities and how each person is predisposed to react.

For example, your extrovert spouse's or boss' primary motivation is the need to feel important. Your spouse or boss wants you to show them why they are important in a very demonstrative and obvious way. Addressing this aspect of their personality will help you understand what the other person values. For example, you could say to your spouse, "I know you feel you don't get enough recognition or appreciation for all you do as a mom/dad/provider. You're out there every day on the front line and we don't know what we would do without you." You could make a similar argument for your boss—minus, of course, calling them "honey."

In contrast, your introvert spouse/employee may want to feel comfortable and at ease—more than just feeling important. We all have these needs. One personality type does not have the exclusive domain on feeling comfortable or important, but the weight that each person gives these needs will vary depending on the personality generalization. If you are uncertain what type of predispositions the other person exhibits, we can look at their role and make an educated guess.

Salespeople in general are more extroverted. Of course, I've known salespeople who act more introverted and don't always like being onstage. However, more than likely if your conversation with someone in sales has gotten off track, the key to righting the ship may involve acknowledging their importance in a direct way. For example, you might say, "Ben, you made your numbers for six months straight. We appreciate how great you are at connecting with customers."

What if you must have a difficult conversation with a service representative? In broad terms, many in this part of the profession tend to be introverts—although they, too, deal with the public. The introverted service rep's primary motivation may be to maintain comfort and ease, even if they disagree or inwardly object to the topic under discussion. The difficulty in dealing with an introvert is to understand that their need to avoid conflict may lead them to stuff their emotions and opinions down deep until they fester. Often, an important message delivered by you or the introvert doesn't hit its intended mark because the introvert wants harmony above all else, which drives the conflict you have with the introverted service rep. Emotions and needs spark conflict as well.

Emotions Matter

Think of a recent uncomfortable situation that you may have faced. Did you move towards or against the issue? What predominant emotion did you feel deep inside? Did you engage in the conversation to move towards resolution or did you move away or try to avoid it entirely?

Moving away from an issue, for those of you that realize that you did, NEVER makes it go away because, as you may recognize, it will come up again and again, ultimately, until it's resolved one way or the other. Thus, if you expect to be successful in resolving difficulty, you can't avoid the conflict entirely.

For those of you that chose to move toward and engage in the conflict, I'd like you to think about the perspective of the other party. Did you know what was going on in their life at the time? Did you consider whether, if the roles were reversed, you would act in a similar way?

Whichever path you choose, engagement or flight, when you look closely, you'll see the elements that were missing that led to the disharmony. Put another way, you'll understand why the other person reacted the way they did—for example, if the introverted service rep felt uncomfortable. Empathy is vital if you wish to move past your own preconceived notions.

There is another possible response to difficult conversations that we haven't yet examined. Often, instead of introspection, we use the natural human response: blame the other party entirely. If you hold stubbornly to the position that you are completely correct and the other party is completely wrong, no progress can be made.

Instead, I'd like you to review the contribution that each of you makes to the discord. In a relationship where there's conflict, I'd like you to remember that it's contributory, not necessarily proportionate. In other words, ***both parties contribute somehow*** in a joint and interactive way. If you've involved in a relationship with someone, then each of you bring a part.

Ask Better Questions

As I mentioned in the chapter on accountability versus responsibility, our personal responsibility is to understand and own our part without focusing on the wrongs or negative contribution of the other party. Remember, we want to be successful in having difficult conversations and resolving conflict in a productive manner. We must be willing to examine our side of the street. I give you some questions that will help:

- What happened?
- What was the result? (Then break out the emotion involved)
- Why did you react the way you did?
- Why do you think they reacted the way they did?
- And be accountable for your part without expectation from them.

Look at the situation objectively. What could be going on? Think about the personality style. Pay attention to verbal cues. Listen to body language. Crossed arms? Fidgeting? Avoiding eye contact?

Did you have an agreement at the end of the discussion? Do you have an expectation that didn't have a solid foundation? After you get clear on these questions, then you can consider what you could have done differently and move into conversation with another party.

A common mistake when talks break down is to gossip and assassinate the character of the other party. Depending on your personality style, you may be more likely to share your side of the story and talk about other people. It's normal, right? We're upset because we have a conflict, and if we're more extroverted, we talk about it and we broadcast it to people, if not simply to proclaim our own righteousness. Human beings are relational creatures and we have a tendency to want to come close to other people to get advice, counsel, and empathy.

The problem is that once you air your dirty laundry, you have a difficult task going back and building relationship. Take heart: If you've crossed this line with others, there may still be room for reconciliation. It depends on how you react to your mistake. You can try another path and, to the degree you can stop reacting to the emotions involved and get some clarity using the questioning process described earlier, you can move closer to resolution. Your first step: Avoid the impulse to make up stories and share it with others.

Coffee with Rick

Remember the story of Jeff and Silvia and the missed lunch? We used that story to illustrate broken promises—but it also serves as an example of the nature of conversation breakdowns.

Let's pretend that you and "Rick" made a lunch date. You both confirmed and agreed Rick was supposed to show up at the coffee shop at noon.

You arrive at the coffee shop early and eagerly wait for Rick to show up. You look down at your watch and notice it's 12:15 pm. Still no sign of Rick. You look at your phone. There is no missed call, no text message, nothing. Ask yourself: How long would you wait before you called him to find out what happened?

You have several responses to this scenario.

a) Text him.

b) Continue to wait.

c) Make excuses for him.

d) Call him to find out what happened.

e) Simply leave and write Rick off as a flake without calling him to find out what happened.

Some people choose option C or E. If that is your response, you may have decided on an explanation that resolves the conflict for you and continued about your business. The picture that you paint would be one that serves your interests and that allows you to resolve your internal conflict. You conveniently take a unilateral action that ignores an investigation that might uncover the reason behind Rick's absence.

To be sure, the nature of the relationship may influence your response. Notice we made no mention of who Rick was in relation to you. If you chose to leave without making a call, would your response change if Rick were your brother? Would you check on him if he were your co-worker, or perhaps your biggest client? What if it was that large prospect you've been waiting months to meet with? Depending on the nature of the relationship, you may reach out to learn what happened. If you don't, you will construct an explanation that suits you and possibly choose to treat Rick differently in the future based on this experience.

By inventing your own explanation instead of asking, you turn inward to resolve the conflict. We often build the story based on our internal belief system—our core. Remember my fictitious example of the Cocker Spaniel? It's natural that we create an assessment, a story, or a judgment in our mind, because that's how we work as human beings.

Examine the themes of the stories you create. Do you create a story that lets Rick off the hook easily? Do you assume the worst—"Rick probably hates me and doesn't want to be seen with me in public"? The story you spin often follows predictable archetypes based on your values and judgments.

For a moment, consider the worst version of your internal explanation. Instead of a reasonable unforeseen circumstance, your assumption is that Rick simply "blew off" your agreed-upon lunch appointment. If that's your story, or your way of resolving your internal conflict without bothering to learn the truth, you will come to several judgments about Rick as a person, just as in the example of Jeff and Silvia. When you describe Rick from that point forward, you'll use terms such as flaky, tardy, and possibly even untrustworthy.

Your tendency may be to simply proclaim, "I'm never going to work with him again," "I'm never going to show up to lunch with him again," or (if he is your brother) "I'm going to avoid him at the next family dinner." As mentioned before, you'll share Rick's transgression around the office, with family or with others in mutual circles (or worse yet on social media).

This may sound like an absurd example, but these situations happen constantly. A more constructive response would be to seek the truth and avoid the tendency to create our own version of the story. In contrast to our negative fairytale, our client or co-worker Rick may have been responding to a family emergency that left little time to notify us of his absence. Thus, the judgments that emerged from our response to this situation may have no resemblance to Rick's true character.

We find it easy to avoid conflict in this scenario: don't ask for an explanation. Thus, by simply creating our own version of the events, we can avoid having a difficult conversation. Instead, I challenge you to make the tough choice and be willing to move toward the conflict in a constructive fashion. Ask difficult questions. The answers may surprise you. The reasons you would have attributed to a scenario based on internal beliefs may be way off target. Don't let your own insecurities keep you in everlasting ignorance merely to avoid risk.

Confronting difficult conversations always involves risk. Many of us feel uncomfortable with the potential for adversity and conflict. However, there's no other way to make progress than to take the bit in our teeth and move toward conflict. Avoidance is the absence of a strategy. The following quote illustrates this concept in poetic brilliance:

"To laugh is to risk appearing the fool. To weep is to risk appearing sentimental. To reach out for another is to risk involvement. To expose feelings is to risk exposing your true self. To place your ideas, your dreams, before the crowd is to risk their loss. To love is to risk not being loved in return. To live is to risk dying. To hope is to risk despair. To try is to risk failure. But risks must be taken, because the greatest hazard in life is to risk nothing. The person who risks nothing does nothing, has nothing, is nothing. He may avoid suffering and sorrow, but he simply cannot learn feel, change, grow, love, and live, chained by his servitudes he is a slave; he has forfeited freedom. Only a person who risks is free."

—William Arthur Ward

For those who may be new at moving toward conflict, some guidelines may help you break your habit of avoidance. Even those who are adept at confronting things head-on may gain some additional insight by applying these principles to difficult conversations.

1. If something that you're struggling with keeps coming up in your mind again and again, you need to be willing to act and have a conversation that moves towards resolution.

2. Remember that there are always at least two perspectives in a conversation of two, not just yours. It's difficult to be open to seeing what's going on for the other party, but doing so will advance your position.

Exercise

I'm going to walk you through a dialogue of difficult conversations and give you some options of what you could do differently the next time this happens. Use the following three concepts to prepare your perspective to have a difficult conversation:

a) Be clear about your purpose. Begin with the end in mind. Author Stephen Covey talked about that all the time. And think of those strange words that I shared with you: "Committed to Create".

b) Ask questions to truly gain understanding of the other person, their circumstances, motivations, and listen to their speech patterns and body language—things that reveal more about them as a person. Are they thinkers or feelers? Are they task-oriented or people oriented?

c) Be willing to shift so that the other person can connect with you. Remember the Brandie-ism, "**I am the only person I can change**." Please be open to shifting, otherwise you will not change the dynamic in your relationships.

Despite your best intentions, the dialogue may break down. Resolving discord happens when you choose to respond differently to the conflict. Begin by examining your part in the breakdown. In other words, did you make and break promises in the past and how have you contributed to the disagreement?

Some tips to keep in mind:

BE CLEAR AND OBJECTIVE ABOUT THE ISSUE AT THE ROOT OF THE CONFLICT. What is the objective issue? Can you look at it without the emotion? When you consider the other party, instead of casting blame, consider what you can do to reassure them that they are being heard. Examine speech, body language, and personality type to address the unintentional blocks that the other party may be stumbling over. With a little thoughtful direction, your actions can bridge the gaps created by the other party. Instead of expecting them to change for you, change your response to work within their limitations if your goal is to find compromise.

TRUE CONFLICT RESOLUTION HAPPENS WHEN YOU HAVE A CLEAR VISION OF AN EFFECTIVE OUTCOME. If you feel uncertain where you want the discussion to veer, you will not be able to make any progress. In other words, go into a situation with clear ideas, at least in your mind, of what you both can do to resolve the matter. Avoid focusing on the other party's transgressions. Don't make it all about them. Admonitions such as "Listen, if you would get it together then we would have a better relationship" do not work.

DON'T BEAT AROUND THE BUSH. Let them know what you want to talk about and that you care about them as a person as well as the resolution of the current issue. Women are notorious for this. "Honey, we need to talk tonight." Poor men. They don't know if that means they're going to get sex or they're going to get divorced! Ladies, please be willing to be clearer without being so vague! Don't go to the other extreme and give a litany of what the other party did wrong. That doesn't help either.

DON'T COMPROMISE YOUR VALUES. Listen for the real issue underneath the conversation. Don't let a disingenuous "Oh, I'm so sorry" defeat you from getting to the bottom of the issue. I assure you that if you do, the same issue will resurface again and again. Move together. Hold true to your values.

PRACTICE, PRACTICE, PRACTICE. Anything new is like driving that stick shift or riding a bike for the first time. You'll grind gears and bump along at first, but soon you'll be a pro at handling the tough challenges when they come. You must be willing to practice this. I know it's so easy when you hear someone like me talk about these things to say, "Oh yeah. I know how to do that," or "Yeah, I've heard all that before." But are you moving beyond your own fear and trying this with the person you can't stand in the office? It's one thing to say, "Yep, I've heard that; yeah, I know that's what I should do," but quite another to invest both emotionally and through action in order to get a resolution. A tip: Use mental rehearsal to practice as well.

THINGS TO EXPECT. It's going to feel a little uncomfortable and you'll feel a little scared to say what you really think. Expect that the dialogue won't go like you planned in your rehearsals, and don't be discouraged. Keep trying. It's better than all the discomfort, anxiety and stress that lurk around an issue not getting addressed.

Here are some great books to help you practice these concepts.

1. Life-Scripts by Stephen M. Pollan and Mark Levine. It's a whole series of conversations that you can have around anything you can imagine in your life and they script it out like the two examples I gave you.

2. When We Say Yes But Mean No by Leslie Perlow. Some of you say yes and mean no. You have a hard time saying no. You don't want to hurt people's feelings. You don't want to step on their toes. You feel like you have a responsibility, a duty to do these things in life as a good person. Then you become overloaded and you neglect the true, important things that you need to be taking care of.

3. Difficult Conversations by Bruce Patton, Douglas Stone and Sheila Heen of the Harvard Negotiation Project.

Your BY WHEN

Think about two specific, challenging stories or situations that you've encountered recently at work or in your personal life. These can be examples of difficult people or difficult conversations that you had.

Did you notice a pattern in the types of people or situations that bother, disturb, or upset you most?

Beyond making it about that person, what are some of the traits that you realized are disturbing you most?

What can you tell about their style, their personality, their way of treating people or talking with people? What are the consistencies?

Think about how you're going to address those items.

Lastly, what's your natural reaction? Who we are under pressure is who we really are and that's a profound statement, isn't it? When things are tough, where do you go?

<u>Takeaways</u>

- Confronting difficult conversations always involves risk. Many of us feel uncomfortable with the potential for adversity and conflict.
- The other party wants to be understood and to be heard as much as we do.
- Moving away from an issue NEVER makes it go away.
- Often, instead of introspection, we use the natural human response: blame the other party entirely. No progress can be made.
- Be willing to examine your side of the street.
- Find out the other person's side of the story.
- Not asking for an explanation allows us to avoid a difficult conversation—and avoid risk.
- There's no other way to make progress than to take the bit

in our teeth and move toward conflict. Avoidance is the absence of a strategy.

- If something that you're struggling with keeps coming up in your mind again and again, you need to be willing to act, have a conversation that moves towards resolution.
- True conflict resolution happens when you have a clear vision of an effective outcome.
- Expect to feel a little uncomfortable.

True conflict resolution happens when you have a clear vision of an effective outcome.

No Donkeys

No Donkeys

We know donkeys for their strength or stamina, but also for their attitude. Donkeys are infinitely stubborn. When someone calls you a donkey, or worse, its genetically superior cousin, a jackass, it's not a compliment.

One of the biggest challenges in organizations is dealing with Donkeys with a capital D, and their executive cousins, the Jackasses—as in the human variety. Rarely do we find any middle-of-the-road solution when confronted with a fully ensconced corporate Jackass. The only way forward is to take a stand and hold your ground while seeking resolution. In life we all have to deal with Jackasses at one time or another.

At a minimum, anyone who confronts a Donkey, whether internal or external to the organization, must answer one simple question: Is it really worth it?

We don't do anyone any favors by hanging onto that client or staying in that unhealthy relationship with a team member, a partner or someone in our personal lives that creates despair everywhere they go. **Yet sometimes we have donkey managers and donkey clients we can't shake.**

In the previous chapters, I've outlined various strategies for change: looking in the mirror; taking inventory; pursuing your dreams; and having a vision. Yet there are some people that are so miserable and unhappy they seek to make every place around them the same way. Unfortunately, some of us remain stuck with them.

Ask yourself, when you have communication logjams that you can't resolve even with all the previous homework you've done, "Do we have a Donkey in our midst?"

If the answer is YES, how do we deal with a Donkey? How do we work with the Jackass if it's part of our job—as a server in a restaurant, a customer service rep or any other occupation? You can't just get rid of Jackasses or refuse to deal with them. However, you can make encounters with Donkeys less painful!

Code Violation List

In organizations that must answer the Donkey question, I suggest a "Code Violation List" for customers. The list includes behavior that the department and the organization find categorically unacceptable. When building a list for your customers, you may include some of the following behaviors:

- Habitually poor payment habits
- A sour impact on the morale of the team
- Demeaning, abusive language
- Consistently poor attitude

You can download our "No Donkeys" decal at www.powerhouselearning.com/NoDonkeys. Post it in your place of business.

You've read the list and you probably nodded while you read it, remembering all the stress from past violations. In my view, no client is worth these heavy prices. No client! Set your standards for the kind of clients or customers you want, as they are indeed **a reflection of you**. Remember that the customer sucks up one team member's time, and also drains precious time spent in other departments, depending on the number of people involved, and the expertise of the men and women of your organization that had to hear the story over, and over, and over again.

Distinguish yourself in offering the best possible use of your team's resources to the kinds of clients you would be proud to work with. Think about exceptional client service and fill your client lists with individuals or companies you are proud to share in your company. Want better client satisfaction statistics? Choose clients with standards that align with yours. Want higher referral lead generation numbers? Pick clients that are a joy and pleasure to do business with and who value what you offer.

You'll still run afoul of code violators. When dealing with them, I find it helpful to discuss client lists in team meetings and to take action to create new agreements with the all-powerful BY WHENs established.

To enact change, address the code violators directly and have the difficult conversation about what's missing in the relationship, and what we can be doing differently to help them better.

You also can say, "In exchange, this is what we need from you, Ms. Customer. We need you to pay your bills on time. We need you to be professionally pleasant when dealing with our team."

If the errant customer refuses to adapt, offer them an alternative to buy from another organization down the street. This counts doubly for Sales and Marketing teams because I know you get paid to bring in customers, and yet if the customers are not profitable, you should not retain that business. My question is, "Are you clear on your 'No Donkeys' approach so that you can see them coming?" Choose to "respectfully decline" to do business with those people or be in personal relationships with those people.

Your BY WHEN

Write down traits of your IDEAL customer, the characteristics of the WORST possible customer, and the WORST possible person to be in a relationship with. What are the kind of people you will stand for and who will you not?

No Donkeys!

Takeaways

- We don't do anyone any favors by hanging onto that client or staying in that unhealthy relationship with a team member, a partner or someone in our personal lives that creates despair everywhere they go.
- Have a list of code violations: poor attitude, late payments, and so on.
- Set your standards for the kind of clients or customers you want, as they are indeed **a reflection of you**.
- The Donkey or Jackass customer sucks up time and energy from the entire organization.
- Think about exceptional client service and fill your client lists with individuals or companies you are proud of.
- You'll still run afoul of code violators—create agreements with them using BY WHEN.
- If the errant customer refuses to adapt, offer them an alternative to buy from another organization down the street.

Create a code violation list for the hiring process, unacceptable employee behavior, current prospects and existing customers. Support your teams by talking about what you will stand for; and what you will not.

How We Handle Adversity Is a Very Big Deal

3

How We Handle Adversity is a Very Big Deal

One of my favorite life principles of all time comes from a series of books by Paul Stoltz on adversity. <u>The Adversity Quotient</u> remains one of my top five favorite books

My takeaway after reading the book: the way we withstand and overcome adversity is a very big deal. Stoltz says that our Adversity Quotient or AQ is greater than emotional intelligence, greater than our IQ in determining our success in life. Our ability to address adversity in life better predicts and defines a positive outcome than what prevailing wisdom would lead us to believe. In reviewing adversity in my life, I discovered that processing difficulty, formulating a response and being clear on what I'm Committed to Create (as well as all of the other principles I've discussed here) were the components that carried me through difficulty. Reading Stoltz's books crystallized this realization for me.

During my toughest times in life, I reflect on the perspective provided by AQ, which helps encourage me during those tense times. I remember that I have all the power to determine my perspective and to be in control of my emotions without letting my thoughts or fears run away with themselves. I have learned to stay focused on the light at the end of the tunnel, no matter how long the tunnel may be! I renew my ability to do what I call "Shake It Off and Take a Step Up," as in the story "The Donkey and the Well" below.

Even though I have a "No Donkeys" policy, donkeys and mules are smart enough to understand adversity, as the following story illustrates.

The Donkey and the Well

Years ago, I had a conversation with someone about why mules are smarter than horses. It's actually true. AND there is a scientific reason why they are so sure-footed and why, if they kick you and miss, they meant to miss! And now on with the story.

One day a farmer's donkey fell down into a well. The animal cried piteously for hours as the farmer tried to figure out what to do. He decided that the animal was old and the well needed to be covered up anyway and that it wasn't worth any of the time or effort to retrieve the donkey. So he invited all his neighbors to shovel dirt into the well to help bury the creature.

At first the donkey realized what was happening and cried horribly. Then, to everyone's amazement, he quieted down and a few shovel loads later the farmer finally looked down the well and was astonished at what he saw.

With every shovelful of dirt that hit his back, the donkey was doing something amazing…he would Shake It Off and Take A Step Up. As the farmer's neighbors continued to shovel dirt on top of the animal, he would Shake It Off and Take A Step Up. Pretty soon everyone was amazed as the donkey stepped up over the edge of the well and trotted off.

You see, life is going to dump dirt on you, all kinds of dirt. The trick to getting out of the well to Shake It Off and Take A Step Up. We can get out of the deepest wells just by not stopping and never giving up!

P.S. The donkey later came back and kicked the hell out of the farmer for trying to deliberately bury him. Which leads to the moral of the story—never try to cover your ass—it will always come back to get you! Author Unknown

Your By When

Learn more about how to relate to adversity when it strikes. Remember who we are under pressure is the person we need to evaluate most.

Takeaways

- How we handle adversity predicts and defines a positive outcome.
- During your toughest times in life, reflect on the perspective in as objective manner as you can.
- Each of us has the power to determine our choices and ability to be in control of our emotions so they do not run away with themselves,
- Renew your ability to Shake It Off and Take a Step Up.

Steps to Reconciliation

4

Steps to Reconciliation

Many years ago the Board of Directors of a large corporation asked me to come in and help diffuse a serious partnership breakdown. The board had been working with the partners for eight months and they were stuck at an impasse. Reaching consensus seemed an impossible goal.

At first, I wasn't sure exactly how to break through the stalemate. As I listened to each side tell their version of the story, I had a moment of inspiration and came up with a four-step process to reconcile these divergent camps and move the organization forward. I'm going to share this simple yet powerful technique that I used in this situation and with many organizations since that time.

STEP 1: RECOGNITION. Until each side can acquire some empathy for the other, and their part in the breakdown, little progress can be made. When both parties are consumed with winning, your disregard the other camp, ignore the nature of the problem and double down on the merits of your position. Please realize that whether you give feedback or receive feedback that defensiveness is a natural reactive response.

STEP 2: RESPONSIBILITY. Each side must own their part in the conflict. We instinctively defend our position and focus on the mistake, which we blame on the offending party. In most situations, this is entirely counterproductive and breeds more hostility and discord. Alternatively, if you encourage each party to own and acknowledge the role they played or actions they contributed to the conflict, something miraculous happens. Each party starts to develop empathy for the other side (Step 1).

STEP 3: COMMITMENT. Very simple. What are you going to do about it? What will you agree to do or refrain from doing? Each party must commit to implementing change and moving forward. It benefits no one to continue to stay stuck. This is a big BY WHEN moment. When I'm involved, we set specific BY WHENS and agree to move ahead without delay. All the hard work leading to this point will be worth the investment as both sides begin to see a way forward and progress becomes possible.

STEP 4: ACCOUNTABILITY. When each side owns its part of the disharmony, meaningful dialogue can then resume. However, it is important to remember that indifference and laziness can derail our reconciliation if we do not call each other out on behavior contrary to our commitment. Equal effort by both parties ensures long-term sustainability.

In my story, when the Board of Directors and partners worked through the steps I outlined above, the dialogue sounded something like this: "I recognize that I've been a jerk, will you forgive me for being that way?" After acknowledgement from the other party, the first party continued, "And this is what I'm going to do about it."

In less than three hours they had broken through some of the biggest items—either that or they were just tired of listening to me talk about it! Either way, it worked. Since that time, they began holding each other accountable as partners with open conversation rather than blame.

I've enacted these simple four steps to achieve reconciliation for many warring factions, be it board members and executives, management and staff, and even in my personal life with my husband. The next time you find yourself in a standoff, try these four steps and begin to move forward.

I would love to report that I've had perfect success in every conflict situation. However, I promised at the beginning that I would be honest with you and share my experience truthfully. I'm going to share one example that didn't go well.

A certain corporation assigned one of their executives the homework of learning my methods and my "secret formula." The corporation asked me to present the concept to management, after which they would use it internally with their staff. Instead, I offered to personally coach the individual who had been assigned to me and walk him through the process with my guidance. The individual reported having a rough time and I thought it better to be personally invested in his success.

After two weeks, he asked me to just give up the formula so he could be done with the assignment. My response was, "Yes, there is a formula and yes, it does work. But it is not the facilitator that should have the victory, rather those who are willing to get down to the core emotions and do the hard work to get the result."

He said, "Well, I have no intention of doing *that* kind of hard work…!"

I had just met a Donkey in Disguise.

If people don't have willingness and open-mindedness little progress is possible. In my consulting practice, I have encountered individuals who were so rigid in their positions that we couldn't make meaningful change. I've found this to be the exception rather than the rule. If you ever encounter a Donkey in Disguise, the best path forward might come at the cost of the party that is unwilling to change—in other words, the other party might break off the relationship. This is a cautionary tale: Don't let that individual be you. The needs of the organization generally outweigh the desire of one individual who wishes to stay stuck.

Keep On Working!

I often tell another story about a CEO standing up in front of his/ her staff saying, "I just want everyone to know that I recognize I've been a horse's ass all year."

During this proclamation, the staff members exchange glances and whisper, "Yup, that's what we say every time you leave the room!"

Then the CEO says, "…and you guys have a great day! You guys keep on a-rowing, keep on a-workin'."

You see the problem with not completing the entire formula? Without all the steps, you can't have true reconciliation. Recognition alone doesn't work. It is a good beginning but what comes after that is more important. Two out of the four won't work. It's one of my secret formulas, and just like any good recipe, it won't work without _all_ the ingredients.

Lastly, a word on how to take feedback when you are being called to Accountability. Allow other people to come forward even if they are not perfect in delivery. If they point something out and you know if your gut that you are responsible, say, "You know what? I can see that, I get it. Thank you for bringing it up." The more times people call you out, the less likely you are to repeat the offense.

The encouragement I want to give you is: if you go through the Four Steps of Reconciliation and you give people permission to call you out, be open to listening when they do. It's tough, because we naturally put up our defenses, especially if our belief system says that honest feedback is an attack. Keep the goal of reconciliation in the forefront and try to be open to critique and be willing to change. The only attitude that can keep you stuck is belligerent denial. Don't be that Donkey in Disguise.

Your BY WHEN

Consider a recent conflict.

Take some time writing and thinking about these four steps and what you can do to create a better relationship.

Takeaways

- Use the process to reconcile parties during a dispute.
- Until each side can acquire some empathy for the other, little progress can be made.
- If you encourage each party to own their part in the dispute, something miraculous happens: empathy.
- What will each party agree to do or refrain from doing?
- Set specific BY WHENS and agree to move forward without delay.
- If people don't have willingness and open-mindedness little progress is possible.

- It's not enough to own up to your part in the conflict. Without all four steps, you can't have true reconciliation. Recognition alone doesn't work.
- Give permission for people to call you out, and be open to listening when they do.
- Keep the goal of reconciliation in the forefront and try to be open to critique and be willing to change.

Try initiating these 4 Steps next time you are involved in a conflict. Are you willing to be humble enough to try it?

Three Big Mistakes Leaders Make

5

Three Big Mistakes Leaders Make

Managers and leaders make three big mistakes in their companies. I've shocked those in positions of responsibility when they learn that their effectiveness within the organization can be greatly improved by focusing these managerial blind spots.

1. LACK OF POWERFUL VISION: Transformation can be very painful—it's change, after all. To initiate change, individuals need to do something different, step out into the unknown, and face fears that everyone has avoided up to that point.

Effective leaders need a vision powerful enough to call people through the pain of transformation. A well-defined vision helps the team get clear and stay clear about the mission and purpose behind the required change. Having clear direction from leadership motivates the rest of the team through the toughest times. When obstacles arise in life, go back to vision and if it doesn't help you or your staff move forward, it is likely that your vision is not powerful enough.

Leaders often fail in making their vision powerful enough to pull the group through the tough times in life. When working in organizations, I ask leaders to walk around the office with $20 bills in their pocket. If someone can stand and recite the vision by heart, they get $20. Another way to keep the vision alive is for people to nominate other people in different departments for vision kudos (make the prize desirable, not some lame gift certificate to the Dollar Store). Recognize ways team members live the vision through interactions with clients, prospective clients, centers of influence, and fellow team members. It often requires concrete reinforcement through simple techniques to determine if the message behind the vision has hit its target. Executives who employ these tactics will quickly determine whether they have a strong enough vision, received clearly by those who are expected to carry it out.

2. LACK OF CLARITY. Most leaders are afraid to be clear. This may seem counterintuitive, but often the person in power may hold back in being decisive to maintain the status quo. Years ago, Fast Company magazine stated that less than ten percent of leaders felt fully adequate in their positions despite a powerful vision from management.

Even with a firm declaration by management, without the right elements and an accompanying set of BY WHENS, oftentimes there is no action within the organization.

Action creates clarity.

Most leaders fail to set a follow-up meeting and homework due at Phase II to solidify the desired position. In sales, we call this necessary work bringing the future to the present. Without the crucial homework, follow-through, and observation of the commitment, employees are unclear about the expectations and change is elusive.

Lack of clarity connects to other human failings:

- Fear
- Self-doubt
- The price you pay vs. what you get
- Not **do**-ing in order to have what you say you want
- Failure to MSU—being frozen

The difficulties that individuals face when implementing change fall on the staff—but the corner office isn't immune. Those in leadership roles must deal with their own insecurities and soundness of purpose to effectively elucidate the vision for the company. First, managers must have that vision and clarity. You cannot transmit something you don't have. Managers and executives must overcome their own personal shortcomings and be unwavering in their commitment to the vision they deliver to their personnel. Don't be afraid to sell your vision!

We often forget the techniques we practice with our customers. Basic relationship training consists of asking great questions and listening carefully to prospects makes the sales process succeed. Good questions and listening skills lead the potential customer along the sales path and allow us to create synergy in our business relationships. What management labels as laziness, lack of awareness, or lack of results on the part of staff is often a reflection of the clarity with which leaders deliver their vision.

3. RESISTANCE TO FEEDBACK A.K.A. THE PINK SHAG CARPET PRINCIPLE: When was the last time you did an internal team survey and an external customer survey? If you did either or both, what dramatic changes did the organization make because of the feedback?

If you can't tell me then your team likely can't either! Employees hesitate to take surveys because they do not see value in the exercise, whether it's for them (leading to positive change) or for their organizations. This attitude is what I call Pink Shag Carpet.

Let's say, for example, you survey your team and discover one lone person in the group wants pink shag carpet. In that case, well, we get them therapy.

But if twenty-five people in the organization openly demand pink shag, you'd better hire an interior decorator!

In other words, if you get overwhelming feedback even if the opinion runs contrary to your own, it is **you** that need to make some changes, **not your staff**. I've observed management's response to surveys in some organizations, and I conclude some people welcome honest feedback, but others, not so much. Often, leaders entirely ignore the feedback given to them in defense of their individual opinions.

Truth time: As a manager or executive, if you ask for and are given honest feedback and don't heed the response, the fault lies on your shoulders. As difficult as you might find working in an office outfitted in pink shag carpet (and you have my sympathy if that's the case), it may be just the item required to move your organization forward.

As I said earlier, some organizations don't know what to do with the survey feedback. Oftentimes they've paid a lot of money in consulting fees simply to question their own employees. These consultant-generated surveys are only a superficial TELLING of information.

It's similar to asking your teenager, "How was your day?"

Standard teenager reply: "Fine."

My question is: Do you really believe them? As a parent, would you just let that go?

If you ask your employees that kind of question and you don't do something you de-sensitize the audience and they stop participating. Let me repeat that: if you ask for feedback and then you don't implement change the employees want, your people will **stop giving you feedback because they don't believe that anything will change.** They will stop giving you the honest answers you need to do better and achieve the goals and the objectives you're trying to attain in the organization.

Instead of seeking change, our natural tendency is to blame someone else for what's missing. When you review the results of the survey, the management team automatically tries to identify the individuals who made the responses. Commonly they will ask, "Who said that?" Often you will hear them answer their own questions: "Oh, yeah, it's got to be the marketing team," or "It's Julie, that sounds just like her."

We encountered this with a group of owners in Atlanta that learned their survey questioned the ethics of the new CFO—no small matter. The group, when reviewing their survey results, said aloud, "Oh yeah, we know who said *that* and she doesn't count."

Upon hearing that response I went further. "Wait a minute, there are four other people who are questioning the ethics of your new CFO and they all work in the same area…"

The response they gave highlighted the problem. "They really don't know what they're talking about. They are all just gossips and don't like him!" They went on, "We like him, and we needed someone in the position."

To deflect attention from the CFO whom they relied on heavily, they pushed the blame on to the other employees. We find it much easier to cast blame onto the respondents than to look at the issues squarely and take the indicated action. Were all of the employees equally questionable or did the owners refuse to accept the feedback they were given?

I left that engagement shaking my head, thinking, "Wait a minute, *something* must be missing here; that is, this many people do not come forward in an anonymous survey in such close quarters in different departments and not have something seriously wrong."

When a company receives honest feedback, unless management is willing to listen and believe in the results without placing blame elsewhere, little change is possible.

Good Leaders

In summation, good leaders are learners who have vision, impart their vision with clarity, and who ask for and receive honest feedback. True leaders do whatever it takes to bring their team along and fulfill the vision they have created. Those leaders that prove to be motivators are clear about what they are "Committed to Create." They focus on "Committed to Create" to help move them into the results they're looking for.

Influential leaders also receive and act on honest feedback and see it as a valuable gift. Treasure honest feedback, because if you have it, it is because your team knows you're willing to make the changes indicated. I congratulate you if you're getting true feedback from your team. Those who receive this rare gift do more than just take the answers and put a check in the box for compliance.

If this sounds like work, guess what: it's **_hard_** work. It takes time, expense, and investment in your people to learn the lessons of true, authentic leadership. And you know what? Here's one of

Brandie's Secrets: those that are doing this are actually getting more production, faster change, and more rewards from their staff. Funny how that works...

Your BY WHEN

Write down at least five things that represent the person that you aspire to be, the person you want to be known as. Now what about your department? Your company? This will begin the process for you of authoring your vision. Once you cement it in your mind, communicate it clearly, follow up, and ask for honest feedback. Overcome your resistance and implement.

Takeaways

- Good leaders are learners who bring their team along, have vision, impart their vision with clarity, and who ask for and receive honest feedback.
- Do you have a vision powerful enough to call you through the pain of transformation?
- When obstacles arise, go back to your vision and if it doesn't help you or your staff move forward, it is likely that your vision is not powerful enough.
- Action creates clarity.
- Without the crucial homework, follow-through, and observation of the commitment, employees are unclear about the expectations and change is elusive.
- The difficulties that individuals face when implementing change fall on the staff—but the corner office isn't immune.

- Managers and executives must overcome their own personal shortcomings and be unwavering in their commitment to the vision they deliver to their personnel.
- Practice the same vision within the organization that you promote to the outside world.
- Don't count on pricey surveys alone by dispassionate consultants to get you honest feedback. They are like asking your teenager how the school day went.
- If you get overwhelming feedback (even if the opinion runs contrary to your own) it is you that need to make some changes, **not your staff**.
- True leaders treasure the gift of honest feedback.
- Brandie's Secret: Those who learn the lessons of leadership are actually getting more production, faster change, and more rewards from their staff.

Leaders must overcome their own personal shortcomings and be unwavering in their commitment to the vision they deliver to their personnel.

Price We Pay for not Taking a Stand

6

Prices We Pay for Not Taking a Stand

Leaders pay many prices for not taking a stand, especially during adversity. Often management knows what action must be taken, but fear rises up as an impediment to the desire to change and push forward. I keep a list of fears that executives have confided to me over the years to explain lack of action:

- Fear of consequences
- Fear of repercussion
- Fear of retaliation
- Fear of a tarnished image
- Fear of losing position
- Fear of looking bad
- Fear of being wrong
- Fear of being less than
- Fear of looking incompetent

A quick survey of this list of fears brings to light the obvious: Leaders are human beings, with essentially the same fears that most individuals grapple with. Being exalted into positions of responsibility often intensifies these fears, because decisions at this level have a ripple effect throughout the organization—or, to put it in executive-speak, there's an increase in securitization of the decisions made by those at the top.

When working with leaders, I find they are often aware of the fears that keep them from moving. Digging a little deeper, I discover they can also list the prices they PAY for inaction. I present a list of responses from executives that illuminates the prices their organization and they personally have paid for remaining stuck:

- Loss of respect.
- Loss of agreement.
- Loss of productivity.
- Loss of camaraderie.
- Loss of feedback.
- Loss of creative energy.

Much as the individual must do in his or her personal life, executives also need to understand what they GET out of remaining stuck. Remember, the price you pay for your entrenched positions does not supply the proper motivation to bring about lasting change. The key to unlocking potential lies in understanding what you GET. Executives candidly reported the following list of what they got in exchange for upholding indecision:

- Comfort in not being judged
- Avoiding difficult conversations with staff
- Dodging responsibility for making the wrong decision
- Evading scrutiny from owners or board members
- Plausible deniability when things go wrong
- Opportunity to place blame on direct reports
- Freedom to pursue outside interests

If you are in a position of power, understanding what you GET out of remaining stuck will shine a spotlight on the areas of your behavior that you will wish to alter. These are the holes in your game. These things keep you from the success and authentic relationships you desire.

Laurie's Story

Laurie in Oklahoma started in customer service and grew into an outside sales role. When we first met, she told me she was at her wits' end because two other people in the office monopolized Jeff, the service person assigned to her.

Even though she moved up the ranks, Laurie felt continually frustrated at the lack of responsiveness from Jeff. In addition to Laurie being agitated, I learned that Jeff planned to quit because Laurie's workload was impossible and she could not follow through on commitments. Laurie on the other hand, felt fed up with Jeff not responding to multiple requests to get things done. Laurie even had examples she shared with me. "Brandie, here's an example: on Wednesday, I gave him some things that needed to get done and on Monday he still hadn't even started!"

My first question to Laurie was, "Did you give him a BY WHEN?" She replied, "No, I didn't. Darn it. And I knew better too."

In our ensuing discussion, I highlighted how BY WHEN helps let Jeff know where to place material in his workflow, and for Laurie it offers peace of mind to recognize that Jeff will have a better chance of getting it done. If Laurie used a BY WHEN, four business days would not have passed in vain.

Laurie proceeded to tell me that the other sales person who gives deadlines gets their tasks completed. Not a surprise.

BY WHEN could make a big difference in the stress level and workload for both employees. We reviewed the necessary requirements when assigning a BY WHEN that there needs to be agreement. Just because we tell somebody what we want and when we want it doesn't mean it will work on their scheduling and on their timeline.

We talked about why Laurie doesn't take a stand with Jeff and worked on her answers to the price she PAYS vs. what she GETS.

I reminded Laurie, "When we assign a BY WHEN, there are three possible answers to our request. YES, NO, and MAYBE, we negotiate. If I don't have an agreement, a definite yes or no, then what we really have is the answer to the math formula Expectations + Reality, which as we know always equals Disappointment. It's vital that Jeff acknowledges the BY WHEN you set and agrees with the terms and conditions you set, even in the simplest of requests. Once you have agreement then you have accountability, or at least a much better shot at it!"

Laurie needed to decide that what she got out of remaining stuck in this situation with Jeff wasn't worth the price she paid. Only then could she set a BY WHEN with Jeff and take a stand.

Your BY WHEN

Think about what it would look like for you to take a stand, to be willing to overcome your fear and achieve the things you say you want in your life.

Consider that you may be judged for this but press through to taking a stand. Acknowledge that change takes time and willingness to go through difficult moments alone, and with those around you. Be serious enough to stick it out.

<u>Takeaways</u>

- Leaders pay many prices for not taking a stand, especially during adversity.
- Fear impedes leaders from following through.
- Executives also need to understand what they GET out of remaining stuck. That is the key to unlocking potential.
- If you are in a position of power, understanding what you GET out of remaining stuck will shine a spotlight on the areas of your behavior that you will wish to alter.

Why People Don´t Move Into Their Goals

7

Why People Don't Move Into Their Goals

"It is a disservice that we ask people to DO something different when the way they RELATE to it is the same."
–Brandie Hinen

The above quote reminds me of a true story about my ex-husband and a little dog named Cricket.

Years ago, I had an awesome hound mix named Gabriele I brought home from the shelter to be a companion to our other dog. However, she liked to wander. No. She liked to flat out take off and RUN into the woods next to our house! After several attempts at keeping "Gabby" in the yard (including an invisible fence), I felt heartbroken when she broke free, darted across a busy road near our house, got hit by a semi-truck and died instantly.

When my now-ex-husband told me about it, I just couldn't believe that it had happened and that she was really gone. I cried non-stop for hours at her loss. The next day, less than twenty-four-hours later, the Ex came home and presented me with a brand-new, six-week-old puppy he purchased from the mall pet store for $700. Did I mention $700 on _my_ credit card?!

The rash purchase aside, I had a problem with the dog. I

thought she was a cute little thing, but not my kind of puppy. Not only that, I still felt grief from Gabby's death the day before. I asked the Ex to take the puppy back, but he was already too fond of her. That little dog whom he named Cricket stayed with him almost thirteen years until she passed away of old age.

While the Ex does earn points for the attempt to help me, it was not a positive experience for me. At least initially. He was ready for a transition and I was not.

Similarly, you can bring someone in to teach a new process, a new procedure, a new way of doing things, but you have to think about what's really going on in the minds and hearts of the people that are being trained. Are they as ready for the change as you are? Remember the chapter "The Consequences of Positive Change."

Look at it this way: You've had time as a manager or leader to think through the process and get your mind around it. However, staff members are proceeding along much as they always have.

We often see management introduce something new and expect their people to be ready to execute post-haste without any warning or preparation.

Instead, consider the emotional state of your team and give your members a chance to talk about the realities of a new process or procedure so that you can design your initiative accordingly. Do not show up with a brand-new puppy and expect your staff to receive it immediately with a warm welcome. Your staff may need time to adapt and appreciate what you are trying to promote.

Executives who take these extra precautions avoid the typical reception of bright new ideas:

- Stonewalling
- Passivity

- Stalling
- Passive-aggressive behavior
- Potential "unintentional" delays

Don't be my Ex. Consider your people.

Your **BY WHEN**

Do you have a new initiative you would like your team to embrace? I hope so! (As learners, we all should.) Take a moment to review the emotional state of your team, in proportion to the change you wish to implement. How should you introduce the concept? What is their history with the current methodology and what obstacles might you have to acknowledge in order to move forward?

Takeaways

- It is a disservice that we ask people to DO something different when the way they RELATE to it is the same.
- Don't introduce change like a new puppy and expect a warm welcome from the team.
- You've had time as a manager or leader to think through the process and get your mind around it.
- Give your members a chance to talk about the realities of a new process or procedure so that you can design your initiative accordingly.
- Your staff needs time to adapt and to appreciate the change you are trying to promote.
- If you prepare your staff, you avoid stalling, stonewalling and potential "unintentional" delays.

COURAGE
CLARITY
CREATIVITY
CHANGE

8

Courage, Clarity, Creativity & Change

Vague, ambiguous phrases that we use in everyday conversation often lead to disappointment. I've identified four of these—not coincidentally, these are areas in which I see breakdowns in organizations and relationships. The opposites of these worthy concepts represent what keeps people stuck and unable to move forward with their goals.

The areas are:

- COURAGE
- CLARITY
- CREATIVITY
- CHANGE

COURAGE

To explain how to have courage, it's more useful to look at the opposite. The opposite of courage is FEAR. When asked what you most fear, surely you can name several things that scare you such as snakes, spiders, etc. But if someone were to ask you where you show the least amount of courage every day when it comes to building relationships or taking a stand for what you believe in, producing a list of categorical courage failings may be harder to construct.

If your largest fear is less socially acceptable, you may resist stating it publicly. In my experience, we often fear the unknown. This manifests as:

- Fear of other cultures or stereotypes of other generations
- Fear of airing a negative attitude or thought about the workplace or coworkers
- Fear of others knowing about an unsavory opinion of one's superior

In business, as you learned previously, we're afraid of looking bad, looking less than, and looking incompetent. These fears have one thing in common: **they all block us from taking risks**. If you wish to grow, you have to take risks.

Courage, Competency and Trying New Things

Courage means just being willing to move, to get your rear in gear. Confidence is knowing you're going to figure it out or work it out somewhere along the way. Stop being so hard on yourself if you don't already know what to do. You're not going to have the competence yet if you're moving in a new direction, because it's uncharted territory. The good news: Your competency will follow as you change your fear into learning experiences. Competency results from facing the unknown and conquering the fear that used to prevent you from movement.

How to Fix Fear

So how do you fix fear?

If you faint in horror at the thought of snakes, immediately signing up for a snake wrangling apprenticeship may be fool-hardy. If the sight of a spider makes your skin crawl, enrolling in Spider Camp may not be the best option for a summer vacation. Trial by fire or jumping in the deep end may suit some people born without a fear gene, but for most people a more measured approach may be more productive.

The following is one of the best practical jokes I ever played on my kids. Thankfully, the statute of limitations has expired for childhood pranking, so now I can share this story freely. The way I see it, my kids got to torment me 364 days out of the year, so ONE DAY out of the year I got to reciprocate, and that was on April Fool's Day.

I was trying to come up with something very creative for my pre-teen, a big arachnophobe. I came up with this Spider Camp idea and I created a really fancy flyer (at least to the eyes of a twelve-year-old boy) using cheesy clipart.

At the time, I had a new voicemail system no one knew the number of yet, and so I put a recording on this voicemail about Spider Camp! Tapping into my best childhood Southern accent, I welcomed my son to an upcoming adventure down in the swamps of Alabama where he would learn to play with spiders, crawl through tubes of spider infested waters, and even learn how to handle the most poisonous of eight-legged beasts!

What fun it was to see his face go white as he listened to the voice mail, opened the envelope with the flyer, and begged me not to send him to Spider Camp! Of course, the amusement was short-lived because I couldn't stand to see him suffer, but it was worth the five minutes of sheer glee. I'm sure he'll have to work the trauma out in therapy or by reminding me about it at family get-togethers now that he is an adult with his own children.

However, at the time, I just couldn't help myself.

So how do you fix fear? Well, you don't just step off the cliff. Some people do and they realize that fear was an imposter. However, for most of us, I find that the way to fix our fear is to focus on a vision that's powerful enough to call us through the pain of transformation and reprogram old beliefs.

How You Will Know You're Still Stuck In Fear

You will know that you don't have a vision that is powerful enough because you will notice that you feel stuck more often than you feel yourself moving in the direction of your dreams. If you feel time slipping away and that you are wasting your talents, look at the vision you have for the future. Look at the direction you'd like to see for yourself, for your department, or for your organization.

CLARITY

The opposite of clarity is vagueness, ambiguity, and uncertainty. If you lack clarity, you will experience emptiness in your business and personal interactions. You will know you have little clarity because you'll feel frustrated within yourself and in your environment. This frustration means that you haven't brought enough clarity to identify what needs to be done, who needs to be involved and what are the problems and obstacles that need to be overcome.

To recap, communication is my least favorite word in the English language, because "lack of communication" really means organizations lack clarity. It also means that a block in one of four communication pathways is responsible for the perceived discrepancy in this popular complaint. I've identified these four pathways:

- Leadership → Staff (staff not receiving the message)
- Staff ←→ Staff
- Staff → Leadership (leadership not listening to staff)
- Department A ←→ Department B

Interestingly, organizations do these surveys to seek direction and clarity but they are afraid to address what the answers mean because the answers are often so vague and ambiguous that management lets it go, which causes more and more problems down the road.

How to Fix Lack of Clarity

Internalize the feedback. In other words, I want you to make it personal. When you receive feedback about lack of communication or not being clear, you need to look at this area personally within your own soul as a human being. How are you connecting with other people?

How You Will Know You're Unclear

You will know if you don't have clarity because you don't see the results from people around you. Think of a boomerang: whatever you give out is what you get back. If you're not clear and specific and you don't set BY WHENS, you will often have broken agreements, which result in broken promises.

Remember when you're getting clear that the feedback for you is personal, so it's a result of something you did or did not say or do. Feedback (especially honest feedback, as I mentioned) is also a precious gift, because you can look inward to find the answers. Once you have feedback, seek clarity by gaining agreement on who will do what and also BY WHEN action will be taken.

CREATIVITY

Teams lack productivity if your workflow, your procedures and your time management aren't going the way you'd like. The culprit? Lack of creativity. Creativity energizes. If you notice a lack of energy around doing something exceptional in your environment, you can change that right away by allowing people to brainstorm and showing them appreciation.

People have amazing minds to come up with ideas and contribute if you will allow them. In fact, I see this with service teams all over the country who seldom receive enough credit for the hard work and creative problem solving they quietly perform daily. Something inspires those teams.

Consider what inspires you in life and in nature, in accomplishing something great and in feeling valued. Ideally, your inspiration doesn't stem just from that one week out of the year when you go on vacation. If the only part of your business that excites you is the absence from your business, you must start getting creative. However, I will say even those who don't consider themselves creative have experienced the rush that comes after a well-spent vacation.

Take that break, and then I encourage you to experience more of life and that exhilaration when you come back into your work environment. Take those feelings that you gain when you were out there and bring them back in and say, "What can we do to interact with one another and see and do things that we never would have done before?"

How to Fix Lack of Creativity

How you fix lack of creativity is to stop focusing so much on RIGHT and WRONG. It's so easy to look at something you see as broken in your environment and focus on what's bad, what's wrong and who isn't doing their job, etc. Instead, move away from those words. Move away from GOOD and BAD and RIGHT and WRONG.

My generation talked a lot about RIGHT and WRONG. I literally took those words out of my vocabulary because I had someone once tell me years ago, "When you make a comparison, someone always has to be wrong!" Of course, no one wants to be the one that is WRONG! If you constantly look at RIGHT vs. WRONG, your focus will be all about what's missing or what's broken instead of how other people contribute.

How You Will Know You've Missed Creativity

You will know if you don't have creativity in your environment because you <u>don't want to involve others that don't think or act or dress or bring ideas according to your tastes and opinions.</u> It becomes a very small, stifling perspective.

<u>CHANGE</u>

What comes up for you when I bring up words like **visionary, daring, exhilarating and exciting**? Think about the victory of creating something very cool that works. People genuinely want new and different things and ideas—that's why we spend millions of dollars a year on self-improvement programs and diet products.

I believe that we are born to learn and grow until we're not here any longer. If you're still breathing that means you have room left for you to learn and change and grow as a person!

For me, change means making a difference for others, to be willing to risk getting outside of my own skin and to be for other people. The status quo of mediocrity is what creeps in when you don't change. It's old and crusty and moldy, as well as static and gross. That's the opposite of change.

Can you think of examples of how you accept the status quo in your organization, department, or life now? I'm sure you can probably list some. And what have you let stop you from doing something great right from where you sit?

Your list of excuses may include: "But Brandie, don't you understand? I'm not that outgoing," "I don't build great relationships," and "I am not comfortable with change." None of that really matters. What matters is that if you see what's missing, you have a power within you to help change the face of things! I believe in you!

What can you start doing now that can be so much better than what you've accepted from yourself in the past?

How to Fix Being Stuck

If you resist change, you are STUCK. Choose to stand out more often and to risk having your own identity. Many of us are tired of the same approach, the same lackluster attitudes of our teams, and lack of authenticity in our interactions.

What do you want to be known for in your life? Move in that

direction. Choose to embrace, with passion, having your own identity. Get out of that rut you recognize you're in. Be known for something. I often think about the question, "What do I want to be known for when I'm gone?"

How You Will Know You Haven't Grown

You'll know if you aren't growing and changing because <u>you will feel way</u> **too comfortable**.

I worked with a very successful real estate developer a number of years ago. After I found out a little more about his situation, I discovered he has grown an incredibly lucrative business. Yet in his early seventies, he did not have anyone to help take over that business.

The person he expected to succeed him did not embrace what was happening or did not see a vision powerful enough, and actually turned in their shares. (Which of course was incredibly discouraging to my owner.) I thought, "You see, it's not that we don't want to change, it's that sometimes we *don't know how to change.*"

So what that owner needed to do, after accomplishing so much in life already, was to be willing to be uncomfortable again to go through the process of change. And in truth, he should have made steps and paid attention to the signals well before his partner left.

I see this scenario often. The businessman in this case has arrived at such a place in life that he worries about how he looks or how people will perceive him. The problem is that he seems pretty foolish when people realize that, in his seventies, he has no succession plan. The only way **through it** is **through it** for him.

He has to be willing to change. He has to be willing to come up with something different and creative and exciting to move him beyond the despair he feels. And I'm sorry to tell you that the only way to move and to create is to **be uncomfortable again**.

It always surprises me when people tell me what they want and how bad they want it in their life. Often, I begin this conversation with a warning that people resist doing the hard work to look inside themselves. CHANGE HAPPENS INSIDE AND NOWHERE ELSE. You cannot expect radical, cool, visionary, exciting and productive growth and not have that work happen within your own body, within your own soul and within your own spirit.

Change must come from within you first. Then, you will have a greater impact on others. Why? Because people are tired of the nonsense. People have become very, very sensitive to lack of genuineness.

Here are some new ways to look at change. See it as an adventure. Act as if you are packing up and going on vacation. You ALWAYS have drama and imperfection on vacation! Someone forgets their underwear or leaves one of the pair of favorite shoes at home. Someone gets poison ivy or someone loses their luggage. You can never anticipate what's going to happen. All you can do is prepare for the best and expect all kinds of obstacles and things coming up in the process.

I know that change is hard, and I've walked in your shoes. I also know what it's like to be on a journey and to have all kinds of adversities and obstacles arise that you never anticipated, and being so caught up in the emotion that you can't always focus on this as being a great adventure. Have people around you that will shake you out of it and say, "Hey! Remember! This is an *adventure* and we've got to keep risking."

What do you have to lose by doing something different? And what do you have to gain? Most importantly, think about what you GET for staying stuck in the destructiveness of change resistance. Be willing to make some tough decisions!

Your BY WHEN

Make a list of projects or conversations you can have with others to talk about COURAGE, CLARITY, CREATIVITY & CHANGE. Use a small project to start. What would it look like to move quickly, swiftly, instead of taking your normal amount of time?

Takeaways

- People can easily identify being afraid of snakes or spiders, but have difficulty identifying where they show the least amount of courage every day when it comes to building relationships or taking a stand for what they believe in.
- In business, we fear looking bad, looking less than, and looking incompetent. These fears block us from taking risks and growing.
- Your competency will develop by attempting new approaches, facing the unknown and overcoming the fears that block you.
- Fix lack of clarity by making the feedback personal. When you receive feedback about lack of communication or not being clear, you need to look at this area personally within your own soul as a human being. How are you connecting with other people?
- Once you have feedback, remember to seek clarity by

gaining agreement on who will do what and also BY WHEN action will be taken.

- Move away from GOOD and BAD and RIGHT and WRONG in judging ideas.
- You'll know you missed creativity because you <u>don't want to involve others that don't think or act or dress or bring ideas according to your tastes and opinions</u>.
- We are born to learn and grow until we're not here any longer. If you're still breathing that means you have room left for you to learn and change and grow as a person!
- The status quo of mediocrity is what creeps in when you don't change. It's old and crusty and moldy, as well as static and gross.
- You'll know if you aren't growing because <u>you will feel way too comfortable</u>.
- See change as an adventure. Act as if you are on vacation. Something unpredictable always happens on vacation!

SECTION IV

BECOMING EXCEPTIONAL

Possibilities Keep Me Sane

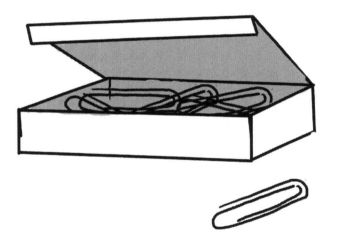

1

Possibilities Keep Me Sane

Pushing myself to see things in new ways, even if I think I have exhausted all possibilities, keeps me moving along life's journey. For creative types, pushing the frontier and suggesting new solutions enhances your effectiveness when going about your daily tasks.

In live seminars, I often play a creative game with the group where we ask people to break off in small teams. Each team has ten minutes to come up with all the possibilities they can for the use of a paper clip other than, you know, its obvious use. It always amazes me to hear some of the creative things that come from this exercise. Allowing creativity to flourish often elicits new solutions to old problems. The exercise can help you if you face difficulty creating your vision.

The exercise highlights several things:

1. We should look at our own abilities beyond our first natural, rehearsed, habit-formed, reaction.
2. Others on the team thought of very witty, smart ideas that you would not have thought of on your own.
3. There is a kind of magic that happens in this energy where you can actually move beyond the limits in your mind at

the onset, and through the exercise of listening to others, actually come up with *more ideas of your own*.

Your BY WHEN

Pick some down time to think about a specific issue you are facing. Can you find a new use for the same old paper clip?

Play a creative game with your group in which people come up with all the possibilities they can for the use of a paper clip other than the obvious.

Takeaways

- Pushing ourselves to see things in new ways, even if we think we have exhausted all possibilities, keeps us moving along life's journey.
- Allowing creativity to flourish often elicits new solutions to old problems.

*When you think of different
possibilities other than your
typical reaction, you open
up opportunities for growth,
breakthrough and relationship.*

LEARNERS
KICK
BUTT

(just not like this)

Learners Kick Butt

Life-long learners share common characteristics that tend to propel them to the top of their respective fields. They learn to listen, watch and interact with others, to check and relate to their responses. They pay attention, remain flexible to modify their behavior, and they use specific follow-ups. Learners apply a formula, and they kick butt!

Have you ever thought about what makes some people stand out from the crowd? Those traits include:

- Desire or passion for their vocation
- Enthusiasm and energy
- Empathy
- Self-esteem / self-confidence
- Positive attitude
- Persistence
- Ego-drive

The following words describe people who possess these four important characteristics.

HIGH ACHIEVEMENT	GOAL ORIENTATION
• Determination • Drive • Passion • Resolve • Persistence	• Clear and specific • Written • Measurable • Achievable • Worthy
EMOTIONAL BALANCE	SOCIAL SKILLS
• Understanding emotions • Even-tempered control • Self-awareness • Ability to deal with rejection • Understanding impact on behavior	• Questioning • Listening • Communication • Intuition • Buying and selling styles

Many of these traits (placed in bold) correspond to learning.

Have you wondered if there are natural born top performers, OR, with the proper training, coach-ability attitude and dedication, that anyone can learn to excel in their given field? Well, people can learn to excel—and again, learners kick butt.

I believe the greatest power is when our knowledge is used to benefit others. In order for that to happen, we must be willing to learn to go beyond the norm and to take initiative even when we don't feel like it or when circumstances are difficult and there is plenty of adversity.

To illustrate this point, let me mention Clinton Anderson, a horse trainer from Australia. He's an exceptional teacher and he brings information in a way that people can embrace it and go back home and use it in every day fashion. He has created an

International following with his methods. I love his quote:

"Frustration begins where Knowledge ends."

In my life, that feeling of frustration is something I try to avoid at all costs. I would certainly rather have the satisfying feeling that I'm moving forward, with the understanding that **there is victory in the struggle,** than the feelings of being STUCK. Those I admire most in life are always in a state of forward momentum. They seek to understand what's going on with the people and processes around them so that they can act with wisdom and empathy.

Through my experiences, I've discovered a repeatable pattern connected with emotions. Invariably, the content I consume that bothers me the most, that triggers an emotional reaction, that disturbs my worldview and rocks some of my limited belief systems, correspond to the areas likely to produce the most growth. After my initial displeasure, I try to uncover why my attitudes and beliefs produce such a pronounced reaction and where applicable, choose to step forward and step in.

While acquiring new information, we can use the same reasoning to uncovering the path to growth.

Your BY WHEN

Write down any areas in your life that you would like to improve on and remember to offset the PRICE I pay vs. what I GET. Remember that if you see life as more of an adventure that you will be more likely to take what comes in stride and be willing to hear the lessons.

<u>Takeaways</u>

- Life-long learners listen, watch and interact with others, and investigate their responses.
- Learners pay attention, remain flexible, and use follow-ups similar to BY WHENS.
- Subject matter that bothers you the most contains the lessons you're avoiding and represents the areas likely to produce the most growth.

"

I don't divide the world into the weak and strong, or the successes and the failures; those who make it or those who don't. I divide the world into learners and non-learners.

There are people who learn, who are open to what happens around them; who listen, who hear the lessons. When they do something stupid, they don't do it again. And when they do something that works a little bit, they do it even better and harder the next time. The question to ask is not whether you are a success or a failure, but whether you are a learner or a non-learner. **"**

~ Benjamin Barber

Counting On A Formula For Success

3

Counting On A Formula For Success

Every time I work with an individual or group of individuals I have a formula, which you know as Committed to Create from Chapter 1 in Section 1. Before my engagement, I go through a mental checklist and prepare to deliver for my audience. My goal is for them to walk away enriched and motivated by implementing my techniques. Without question, I believe it is my soul's purpose. When I deliver a message, I create an experience based on the needs of my recipients, and based on the purpose of presence:

- Understanding the reason for the meeting
- Being clear and evoking clarity
- Considering the other
- Paying attention to verbal and non-verbal feedback
- Delivering what they perceive as value (not what I perceive)
- Creating agreement
- Using BY WHEN

This is the formula and I have used it for many years. Through practice, I have made it a subconscious effort.

I highly recommend the book The Go Giver by Bob Burg and John David Mann. Their "5 Laws of Stratospheric Success" have helped remind me of similar principles I endeavor to live by as well.

Many people ask me, "How can you walk into any situation with anyone in the company and move people the way you do?" Or, "How can you stand in front of hundreds of people and engage them the way you do, allow them to bring up different scenarios, take questions from an audience, and then circle everything back around and have it all make sense?"

The answer is that I count on my own little formula. It works for me *every time* and helps me stay centered and focused on my vision for making a powerful difference in the lives of those I encounter.

Your BY WHEN

Create your own Formula for Success by first defining what success is for you. Then identify what (a) skills, (b) traits, and (c) knowledge you will need to develop to be exceptional in your field. Who can you serve to help you achieve what you say you want? What habits or nuances do you need to shift in order to have more control over your circumstances?

Takeaways

- When I work with an individual or group of individuals I bring a formula for success. It works for short term situations and my long term vision.
- Through practice, this formula can become a part of you (subconscious competence).
- The formula is always other-focused.

*Taking a hard look at
areas to grow personally
and professionally will
help further your personal
definition of success.*

KEEP YOUR STRATEGY MOVING

Conclusion

A Final Thought: Keep Your Strategy Moving

I often hear people talking about plans and execution of those plans, but they often miss the mark when they hit the first brick wall, the first obstacle, a negative judgment about the person proposing the plan or the first fifty unread emails when they return from the meeting! This happens all the time after Strategic Planning sessions.

Does everyone know what is expected in clear terms and what will be done when Plan A does not go perfectly?

I often say we do not plan for the third BY WHEN. We only think of the first in vague terms like "by the end of the week" or "sometime in the third quarter."

In order to keep your strategy moving, you must anticipate **FAILURE**.

Plans and goals need to include simple written dialogue on these topics:

- How will you know you're ON track?
- When will you know that you are OFF track?
- What will you do when you realize you are OFF track?
- How quickly will you course correct?

Let's say that we're working on a goal or an initiative in the department and we realize that we're not getting the results we're looking for. In that moment, ***as soon as you recognize the gap in results***, you decide to move and change without delay. Hoping and wishing won't fit the bill.

Call an all-hands meeting and say, "Look! We can gloss over this or we can wait for more lack of results, but we agreed that if any of us recognized we're not on track, that this is where we needed to course-correct." By outlining this contingency ahead of time, people and organizations get results a lot faster. It creates rigor in the communication style and creativity towards moving into the results.

I share this simple little piece with you last because it is one of the most important. **Implementation is key to success, to moving from Discussion into Action and to becoming the person you are meant to be.** Sitting safely in your pajama pants with a philosophy about how things should be or affecting others with your bitterness, negativity and cynicism because things aren't going the way they should in your life doesn't further your expedition. If it were that way, internet trolls would be awarded Nobel Prizes.

All of us face tough times and adversity, but the victory is to the overcomers. I encourage you to stay on the course of learning, be aggressive in your quest for knowledge, and be humble in your victories and contemplative in your defeats.

Parting wisdom and Brandie-isms:

"We have been conditioned to accept philosophy
without action as innovation."

"It is a disservice that we ask people to DO something differently
when the way they RELATE TO IT is the same."

"We judge ourselves by our intentions and
everyone else by their actions."

"When you have Agreement you have (better) Accountability."

"It always surprises me when people tell me what they want and
how bad they want something different in their life, then they
resist doing the hard work to look inside themselves. Inside is
where change happens and nowhere else."

"BY WHEN…"

Acknowledgements

My heart is filled with gratitude to those close individuals in my life that have loved me through this process. First and foremost, to my sweet husband, Jim, who has infinite patience for my bold way of seeing the world. Next, to Greg Easley, Justin Fowler and Allison Throckmorton who would not let this idea die despite my hesitancies, but instead have cared enough to push me forward.

Super amazing props to my creative illustrator, web master, and Disenarte, Juan Ramón Morales, info@diseniarte.com. Thanks to Aimee Mosco, www.ihsunity.com, for your never-ending love and gifted intuitive insight (and for the referrals to my editor Kristin, www.kristinjohnson.net, and designer, Deborah, www.tugboatdesign.net.)

Lastly, I also want to thank those over the past decade who have asked for a book. The memory of their faith in me was not forgotten.

Biography

Brandie Hinen is the dynamic transformation coach and founder of business consulting and coaching firm, Powerhouse Learning, as well as an influencer on LinkedIn with over 400,000 followers. Those who work with Brandie experience a sense of motivation to try new things, authenticity in their resolve, and the victory of achieving their goals and vision as she brings real-world ideas and processes that help transform the lives of those she works with. Brandie is an accomplished instructor, trainer and expert on how to move people from Discussion into Action. Born in the South, she experienced a diverse childhood with international travel, developed a lifelong love of learning, and by demand, embarked on that strange career named Consulting where she engages in dynamic conversations with fellow learners every day. She currently lives in Boise, Idaho with her husband and miniature bull terrier, Joia.

To learn more about Brandie and her team at Powerhouse, check out www.PowerhouseLearning.com or Brandie Hinen's LinkedIn page.